WHAT THEY'RE SAYING ABOUT "FATHER'S DAY MIRACLE"

The book had me at "Cleveland sports fans." Any book that combines fatherhood with the love of sports will be a great read, but what sets "Father's Day Miracle" apart is its ability to help me be a better father, to go far beyond sports to what really matters: impacting the lives of my children.

~ **Greg Nettle, President of Stadia; Co-Author of "Small Matters: How Churches and Parents Can Raise Up World-Changing Children"**

The miracle of fatherhood is the only thing that tops the "Father's Day Miracle." These intimate accounts of the challenges and rewards of being a father are guaranteed to stir up a fresh sense of commitment to raising spiritually and emotionally healthy children.

~ **Pastor Jerry Birch, Team Chaplain, Cleveland Cavaliers**

If victory has a thousand fathers, then no wonder LeBron and his Father's Day Miracle have a million of them, literally. After reading through this series of stories, I knew I had to own this book, read this book, and share this book. Your story is also hidden within these pages. CLEVELAND, this is for you!

~ **Ray Jeske, Host, "The Ray Jeske Show," ESPN 990**

If you're a coach, pastor, dad or Cleveland sports fan, this book is for you. You hold a position of great influence and what you do with that influence has the power to impact generations to come. The stories in "Father's Day Miracle" are powerful and convicting – enjoy!

~ **Hannah Calhoun, Area Director,**
NE Ohio Fellowship of Christian Athletes

Fathers have the power to impact their children in profound ways. These stories vividly illustrate the ways kids thrive when their fathers are present and engaged in their lives and, sadly, the ways they struggle without that male influence to provide guidance and direction. We have been delivering programs to assist fathers in meeting both the financial and emotional needs of their children for the past 12 years and have seen the significant difference it makes when children have a productive relationship with their fathers. "Father's Day Miracle" will inspire all dads to invest in their kids and commit themselves to a better future for their families.

~ **Al Grimes, Director, Cuyahoga County Fatherhood Initiative**

This book highlights the importance of perseverance and patience in the sports arena. The same is true in fatherhood. We must persevere as dads to love our children the way God loves us. And we must be patient with them through those tough years, just as our Heavenly Father is patient with us. I love how this comes through in the stories in this book!

~ **Kent Evans, Executive Director, Manhood Journey**

June 19, 2016 – Father's Day – will forever be remembered by Cleveland sports fans as the night our team won the big game and became champions. The stories in "Father's Day Miracle" highlight that amazing night but, more importantly, encourage dads to be champions in the lives of their children.

~ **Steve Sanders, Cleveland Metro Director, Fellowship of Christian**
Athletes; Chaplain, Cleveland Cavaliers; former Cleveland Browns WR
(2006-08)

"Nothing is given. Everything is earned." Those words from LeBron James became Cleveland's official mantra, but the stories in "Father's Day Miracle" draw an obvious parallel to fatherhood. Mistakes in life are inevitable, but whether you're overcoming them on the court for your hometown, or doing so in your home for the betterment of your family, it's all a victory in the end.

~ **David Regimbal, Lead Ohio State Football Writer,**
   Bleacher Report (8/2012 – 2/2017)

Many of us had great fathers who challenged us to live our lives as influencers for Jesus, but others didn't have a father to teach what it means to be a man. "Father's Day Miracle" offers fascinating examples of both. I would venture to say that disengaged fathers have contributed to many of the problems we see in today's world. If men are the problem, then men have to be the solution as well. I hope you are inspired to use this book to help the men under your influence live out their lives as agents for good in the world.

~ **Todd McIntyre, Gateway Men's Pastor, Southlake, Texas**

To fathers everywhere who have taught their kids how to "reach into the cookie jar" on their jump shots, how to throw spirals and curveballs, and how to hit their irons and read a green; especially those dads in northeast Ohio who kept the faith despite the losing and somehow managed to pass their love for our teams down to the next generation.

FATHER'S DAY
MIRACLE

Faith, Fatherhood and the Day
Everything Changed for Cleveland Sports Fans

Father's Day Miracle
Published by One Heart Communications
oneheartcommunications.org

In partnership with:
A Book's Mind
PO Box 272847
Fort Collins, CO 80527

Copyright © 2017
ISBN: 978-1-944255-44-2
Printed in the United States of America

Scripture quotations are from the ESV® Bible (The Holy Bible, English Standard Version®), copyright © 2001 by Crossway, a publishing ministry of Good News Publishers. Used by permission. All rights reserved. Unless otherwise indicated, all Scripture quotations are from the ESV® Bible.

CONTENTS

PREFACE

"Wouldn't it be incredible if they actually won it on Father's Day?"

The question hung in the air, neither of us particularly eager to answer. We're Cleveland fans, after all.

It was Friday, June 17, 2016, and the administration building on the Wooster, OH campus of Christian Children's Home of Ohio (CCHO) was buzzing. Many of us had shown up that morning in our Cavaliers t-shirts, bleary-eyed after staying up late the previous night watching our team nail down a 115-101 victory in Game 6 of the NBA Finals to tie the series with the Golden State Warriors at three games apiece.

Game 7 loomed. Just over 48 hours until tipoff. Father's Day.

History hung in the balance. A win Sunday would mark the first championship in franchise history for the Cavaliers. It would also make them the first team ever to win the NBA Finals after trailing in the series 3-1. And – lest we forget – a victory would bring the city of Cleveland its first major sports title in 52 years. So many possibilities, just one game.

Our feelings swung back and forth from wild excitement to jittery anxiety. For any seasoned Cleveland sports fan, there was no middle ground. We'd seen big games before and five decades of data indicated that this one would end the way the others had: in heartbreak.

You'll have to excuse the bleak outlook but we Cleveland fans had earned our pessimism while enduring moments in sports history that merit their own Wikipedia entries. The Drive. The Fumble. The Shot. The Decision. And as if Art Modell ripping the Browns out of the city and relocating to Baltimore in 1996 wasn't painful enough, we watched in agony a year later as the Indians coughed up a ninth-inning lead in Game 7 of the World Series before ultimately losing the series in extra innings.

Our teams not only had barren trophy cases, but on those rare occasions when they actually came close to bringing the city that elusive championship, they took turns authoring painful losses on the biggest stages.

So when we considered the possibility of the Cavaliers ending 52 years of misery on Father's Day, it seemed far-fetched and yet, in many ways, very fitting.

Fathers have been passing sports legacies down to their children for generations, with team allegiances representing cherished family heirlooms that endure regardless of what the standings say or whose names are on the backs of the jerseys. Loyalty to a team is just that: sticking with an organization no matter the circumstances, no matter the results, no matter the history, no matter what.

For many families, this sports heritage runs deep as they continue cheering for their hometown teams, generation after generation, through winning and losing seasons alike, simply because "Dad did."

But in Cleveland, all "Dad did" was root for teams that seemed to compete with one another in search of the most devastating ways to disappoint their loyal fans. Those crushing Wikipedia moments would come to define what it meant to be a modern Cleveland sports fan as northeast Ohio became synonymous not just with losing, but losing in historic fashion. "OIC," the fans would mutter in the wake of each disappointment: Only in Cleveland.

While the collection of unfathomable losses only made the joke that much funnier to outsiders, the Browns, Indians and Cavs started losing younger generations of fans who never watched Brian Sipe or Bernie Kosar sling the ball around Municipal Stadium; who never saw Joe Carter or Jim Thome smash a home run deep into the outfield bleachers; who never heard of Mark Price or the Miracle of Richfield and whose most vivid memory of LeBron James was when he left for Miami. Fathers tried to pass down the love for Cleveland sports that they had inherited, but all their kids saw was the heartache and frustration that came with it, convincing many to find other teams to follow or to ignore sports altogether.

And yet, Dad kept cheering. Despite the losses, despite the national punch lines, long-suffering Cleveland fans endured, sustained by an unshakeable faith that the narrative would eventually change and the decades of futility would make that first title taste even sweeter. "One day," Dad believed. "One day."

Could "one day" actually be Father's Day?

The question kept rolling around in our heads that Friday afternoon. A Cavaliers win on Father's Day wouldn't just be a great story; it would be history, for the NBA, for the Cavaliers franchise, for the city of Cleveland and for its title-starved fans. It would, in short, be a miracle.

The name was born, and, though we didn't know it at the time, so was this book: "Father's Day Miracle."

A couple hours later, we had a domain: **fathersdaymiracle.com**. We didn't know what we were going to do with it, but we had it.

Ideas started percolating that weekend, leading into Sunday morning, and we kicked around trying to create some merchandise for Father's Day Miracle that celebrated the Cavs' championship. But there were two problems: We didn't really have the time or even the desire to make and sell t-shirts, and – oh, yeah – the Cavs hadn't won anything yet. The game hadn't even tipped off!

We enjoyed Father's Day morning and early afternoon with our families but the idea wouldn't go away. Eventually, we landed on one word: stories.

After 52 years of waiting, we knew a win that night would be one of those moments that Cleveland fans would not only remember forever, but would tell stories about for the rest of their lives, with intricate details from the day permanently carved into their memories.

So, with mere hours to go before the game, we set out to capture some of those would-be stories by creating a Facebook page and launching a blog that would allow fans from across the world to share their "where were you when" moments with one another. If the Cavs won, we thought people would have a blast reading the "Father's Day Miracle" stories from fellow fans and posting their own.

If they lost? We never would have spoken of it again.

Spoiler alert: They didn't lose. Despite heading into halftime down seven points to the Warriors, the Cavaliers stormed back in the fourth quarter to chase down history and end the night with an epic four-point win. Father's Day Miracle: complete.

Northeast Ohio predictably erupted, overcome with feelings of both unbridled euphoria and overwhelming relief. The streets were filled with revelry; cell phones were blowing up all over the state; Facebook feeds were clogged with photos and videos of fans celebrating the moment. After more than five decades, this victory really did taste that much sweeter. The narrative had forever changed. "OIC" had an entirely new meaning.

Fathers who had only heard stories about the 1964 Browns or the Indians' 1948 World Series title now had their own championship memory to share with their kids, a Father's Day Miracle that revitalized the Cleveland sports heritage. Rooting for Dad's teams no longer meant rooting for losers. Decades of loyalty despite all the heartache finally paid off.

So, of course, fathersdaymiracle.com exploded with activity as fans rushed to our site eager to share their stories, right? Well...no. Some people found us on Facebook that night and we had a couple stories like this pop up on the blog in the days that followed:

"I couldn't turn off ESPN last night. I wanted to hear everyone talk about a Cleveland team finally winning it all. I soaked it all in. When I finally dragged myself upstairs well after midnight, I wondered what I would feel like in the morning. I'm so used to waking up on the day after games like this with an empty feeling in my stomach, knowing the season was over, the dream had died yet again, and it was time to wait for next year. It's a feeling all Cleveland fans are used to waking up with and then carrying around for months. Today? Today, we woke up with a far different feeling. It's finally next year, Cleveland!"

In hindsight, while the idea was good, it admittedly was unrealistic to expect people to write more than a sentence or two for that kind of project, even for something as incredible as this. Ah, but what if we didn't wait for those stories to find us, and instead tracked them down? And what if those stories were about more than just sports, but instead delivered a greater message about the tangible, intricate and sometimes even complicated impact sports have had on generations of families in general and fathers in particular?

And finally, what if those stories looked at it all through the lens of faith? As men of faith ourselves, we try to filter everything in our lives through the relationship we share with Jesus Christ, and our families naturally sit at the top of that list. Beyond that, though, we see firsthand the damage done when fathers are not involved in their children's lives through the work we do with our family of ministries: CCHO, Encompass Christian Counseling, and Encourage Foster Care & Adoption.

While the Cavaliers – or, really, any Cleveland team – winning a championship seems miraculous, we know our Heavenly Father authored the biggest miracle of all on the cross more than 2,000 years ago. In addition to celebrating one of the greatest moments in Cleveland sports history with this book, we wanted to illustrate the impact fathers make when they fully engage in the lives of their children while creating awareness for the importance of foster care and adoption to kids growing up without these vital relationships.

After much prayer and discussion, what we ultimately landed on is what you're holding in your hands right now: a collection of stories formed on that historic day at the intersection of our calling as fathers, our passion as Cleveland sports fans and, above all, our identity as followers of Christ. These writers all have very different stories to tell, but each of those stories thoughtfully and honestly explores the themes of faith, fatherhood and fandom. The result is a book that celebrates fathers while acknowledging that none are perfect; that commemorates one of the most joyous moments in Cleveland history while examining why sports matter so much to so many people; and that praises the work that God has done in our lives simply because He loves us – fully, wonderfully and unconditionally.

All proceeds raised through the "Father's Day Miracle" project will go directly to Christian Children's Home of Ohio as we continue to help at-risk kids who are often abused and neglected find hope and healing in our Children's Residential Center in Wooster, OH. Our mission at CCHO, Encompass Christian Counseling, and Encourage Foster Care & Adoption is to help introduce people to their Heavenly Father so they can find their true worth, many for the first time, in a lasting relationship with Jesus Christ. We are excited to see how God will use these stories and this project to show more of His children just how much He loves them.

To learn more about our family of ministries and to support our mission:

ccho.org
encompasscounseling.org
encouragefostercare.org

1 STEPPING INTO THE GAP

By Gary D. Porter
Retired former Executive Director, Christian Children's Home of Ohio

"Father of the fatherless and protector of widows is God in his holy habitation. God settles the solitary in a home; he leads out the prisoners to prosperity, but the rebellious dwell in a parched land."

Psalm 68:5-6 ESV

My days with the Cavaliers started in 1974, in the middle of a field in Richfield Township, between Akron and Cleveland, with the building of the Coliseum by businessman Nick Mileti. When the Coliseum was finished, Nick held an open house before any games were played there, inviting everyone to come and tour the new facility. I attended that open house and was blown away: It had easy access from the interstate, easy parking and top-notch everything. It was also so close to my home in Akron. I couldn't wait to see the Cavs in their new home arena.

The Cavs were only in the league four years when they moved to the Coliseum. The team's biggest rivalries were Boston, Detroit and, of course, the Chicago Bulls in the Michael Jordan era. These games were as intense as any rivalries today. We faced some tough and aggressive players in Detroit, such as Dennis Rodman, Rick

Mahorn and Bill Lambeer. The Pistons were known as the "Bad Boys," and I saw more contact against them than I did in most Browns games. I remember Jordan hitting "The Shot" over Craig Ehlo...but first I remember Jordan pushing off to get the shot.

We always had quality players on and off the court: Larry Nance, Brad Daugherty, Austin Carr, Mark Price.... These were players you didn't mind being role models for our children. I attended several events where Price was the main speaker, with one such event being held at First Christian Church in Canton. Well over a thousand were blessed that day by Mark sharing his faith and his desire to see his popularity bring glory to his Lord Jesus Christ.

I visited the Coliseum countless times with my family, church groups, and many children and staff members from the Christian Children's Home of Ohio (CCHO). It was always great to take children who had never been to a professional game and watch them root for the Cavs. We have cheered for the Indians and Browns as well, but those days were largely marked by disappointments, watching the few genuine championship dreams we had get crushed in the final moments of close games. Still, even those times allowed our family to get together and cheer for our teams.

I have three children who have their own families now, and I have five grandsons. Even though my youngest child is 41 and we live in three different states, the entire family was together on a family vacation at the beach for the 2016 NBA Finals, so we were all together to cheer on the Cavs. What perfect timing: Cleveland finally won and we all celebrated together. What a feeling! Being with family made it all that much better. Being a father trumps being a fan every time.

And that is a central truth in our lives. We did things together and family was foremost. We supported each other. I remember attending a lot of wrestling matches, volleyball games, basketball games, track meets and softball games when my children were in high school. When they were in college, we would drive five hours each way to see a basketball game and volleyball matches. When I would be traveling throughout Ohio speaking at various churches, my family was with me. I am sure each of my children could have made the presentation regarding CCHO if for some reason I couldn't. We are family.

My five grandsons range in age from fifth grade to a college sophomore, living in three different states. They are involved in soccer, hockey, track and cross country. There are some long trips (four to five hours) to see them compete, but I wish we could do even more.

Why is being a dad and grandpa so important to me?

Let me tell you about a little boy born to a single mom in a small Ohio River town in 1945. It was not a pleasant time for him or his mom. She was ostracized and shunned by most people in that community and treated like dirt. It was rough on the boy as well, as he heard unpleasant things about his mom while being called names most of his childhood, all of which led to fights. Lots of fights.

His mom took him to church each Sunday, which was hard on her. You see, she used to be the church pianist until she became pregnant, and then that was taken from her. But she knew that in that little church were some good men who might care about her son. She was right: They did care, and they taught him Sunday school for nearly 20 years.

Then something happened that would change that boy's life forever: A new minister named Grant Layman came to that small church. Grant would become a surrogate father to the young boy who never had a dad. This young minister showed this young boy more love than anyone other than his mother had. The boy soaked it in and began to grow in his faith, accepting the Lord and getting baptized at age 12.

He began to feel more accepted and he would stop by to see Grant almost every day at the church. With growing confidence and encouragement, this young man began to play baseball and Grant came to many of his games. As he got older, he tried out for and made the high school basketball team. Once again, Grant came to the games and filled a hole in this young man's life where his father should have been.

Grant was there when this young man went forward on a Sunday at church and dedicated his life to full-time Christian ministry.

The young man was growing up, working some, trying to help his mom. One day after some prayer and some really deep breaths, he went to see his birth "father" who lived two hours away. This man owned a large company and his mom needed $100 to buy some coal to keep the house warm. The man gave him nothing, cussed him out and threw him off his property. He was crushed.

After graduating from high school, he did what most young men in the valley did: He went to work in a steel mill. After about a year at that mill, Grant asked the young man to stop by the church office after work. When he did, Grant reminded him of his commitment to full-time ministry. The young man did not know what to do because he had no money to even consider college. This man of God replied, "You need to go home and get ready because you need to be at Milligan College in seven days. Everything is taken care of." Grant had graduated from Milligan many years earlier.

The young man and his mother were shocked, but in seven days, this young man was on the campus of Milligan College in Tennessee.

At Milligan, he found so many more men of God who "adopted" him, and in four years he graduated with dual majors of ministry and psychology, and began working as a youth minister back in Ohio. Grant was there when he graduated and he also performed his wedding ceremony. A REAL FATHER.

That little boy from the Ohio Valley praises God everyday for the surrogate fathers who loved him and poured their lives into him. And I am doing okay today. I was awarded the Distinguished Alumni award from Milligan College, I served on their Board of Trustees and I have now been married for 50 years, the father of three children and grandfather to five. Give praise to God.

I also recently retired as the Executive Director of Christian Children's Home of Ohio. My heart was and still is to take care of the fatherless. Two of the most exciting events for me in my 33 years at CCHO were those times when we saw a child adopted into a new life with a Christian family and when we saw young people give their lives to Christ.

I still love sports in general and the Cavaliers in particular. I have in front of me a sports card of LeBron James in his St. Vincent-St. Mary uniform back in high school, the front pages of the *Akron Beacon Journal* and the *Plain Dealer* from the day LeBron announced that he was coming home, and an 8"x10" photo in my office.

I will always have a soft spot for the Cavs, but I prefer the 8"x10" family picture with all 13 of us gathered for Christmas.

ABOUT GARY PORTER

I have been blessed to have ministered to children for 43 years (33 of those with CCHO) and to still be involved with a ministry to children in Ukraine that we helped start 18 years ago. *"Let your light so shine before men that they may see your good works and glorify your father in heaven." (Matt. 5:16)* I pray my life has reflected this passage from Matthew. I wrote to share my story with the hope that other Christian men might find another lonely boy to help along the way, just as Grant did for me.

2 COME WITH ME

By Dave Jamerson
Lead Pastor, Renovate Church Austin; former NBA first-round draft pick

"For the Lord reproves him whom he loves,
as a father the son in whom he delights."
Poverbs 3:12 ESV

I probably didn't know it at the time when I was growing up in the Akron, Ohio area, but I had it really good.

My father, a terrific basketball player in his own right, was always there for me. He would just say, "Let's go play this afternoon," and we would spend hours shooting hoops while he taught me everything he knew. In a way, it was my first introduction to the whole idea of discipleship. More about that later.

Dad was a star player at Fairmont State University in West Virginia, and was drafted by the Indiana Pacers of the old American Basketball Association. He would eventually wind up playing for the Akron Goodyear Wingfoots, and our long-term love affair with Cleveland sports began. We were there for "Red Right 88" in 1981 when the Browns were upset by Oakland. We were on the edge of our chairs, dying a slow death when "The Drive," "The Shot" and "The Blown Save" happened to us.

Yes, it all happened to us. Cleveland is like that. Diehard fans whose hearts break with every close call and every loss.

And, then, the 2016 Cavs won it all, and all was right with the world. My dad and I talked after every game and rejoiced in the final outcome.

MY OWN BASKETBALL STORY

Long before I had the opportunity to play in the NBA, my father saw it and believed it could happen, and told me so. Though I was only 5'11" and 140 pounds, he saw me as so much more. At that time, my sophomore year in high school, I loved baseball and I loved football, and I sort of tolerated basketball. But then, between my sophomore and junior years, I had a growth spurt, and when I came back for my junior year, I was 6'3". I began to pay more attention to basketball, and I went out that year and had a pretty good season, averaging 14.6 points a game on a 19-3 team.

That summer, things changed even more dramatically. I attended Five Star Basketball Camp, a top basketball camp with the best high school players from around the country, and I had an amazing run. I was the second leading scorer there and made the all-star team. My phone started ringing with college scholarship offers, and I could see right away that playing every night in front of college scouts could be a distraction.

So, I made a strategic decision, one that seems pretty mature, looking back at it now. I took some visits to several interested colleges, and then went to visit Ohio University (OU). As soon as I drove onto the campus, I knew: This was the place I wanted to be. The campus was beautiful and the basketball team was on a terrific run of success. Plus, it was only a few hours from home – close enough to get back if I needed to, and far enough away to let me start growing up a bit.

I wound up signing with OU, and then I went back home and had a dream season, averaging 34 points a game for our 20-0 undefeated team. I felt ready to bring my skills and talent to the college game. In fact, I looked forward to it.

OHIO U AND AN UNEXPECTED CRISIS

My freshman year, I was the sixth man during what would be another good season for the Bobcats, coming off the bench to average 14 points per game. All in all, a good start for me. I really liked this team. The chemistry was terrific, and it was a lot of fun to get out there and play in front of thousands of people, all packed into our 13,000 seat arena, all raising the roof for every good thing that happened.

I was living the life.

The team went over to Europe that summer to do a series of exhibitions and before leaving for our trip, I picked up a copy of *Sport* magazine. Inside, they ranked the best college players in the U.S. Much to my surprise, they had me as the #5 best shooting guard in the country. I was on cloud nine.

The European exhibitions went well, too. I averaged a little better than 30 points per game and I was really in the zone as we crisscrossed the continent. It was a heady experience, and a bit surreal for me.

And, then one night – one awful night in Holland – an opposing player tripped and fell through my knee, totally destroying it.

I flew back home and met with doctors. The prognosis wasn't good. I had torn ligaments. I would have to miss that entire season, and the doctors wondered aloud if I would ever be the same player I was before the injury.

In just a matter of a few hours, I went from the highest high to the lowest low. But, as is always the case when trouble comes calling, there were lessons to be learned in my difficult moment. First of all, I realized that neither I nor basketball were the center of the universe. Secondly, I had so much of my identity wrapped up in basketball and sports in general, I began to ask the questions that would eventually lead me to my faith: Is this all there is? Who am I really? What if all of this was taken away?

HAKEEM AND JESUS

Well, the doctors' concerns about my future as a player turned out to be inaccurate after all: I rehabbed successfully, and in my sophomore year I averaged 17.3 points per game. I didn't feel like my old self for much of that season, but then toward the end, I settled into a groove and raised my game to a new level, even above where it had been before the injury. That strong finish propelled me into my junior year, when I averaged 19 points per game. The stage was set for my final season in Athens.

Now two years removed from my knee injury, I exploded during my senior season, scoring more than 31 points per game. My draft stock soared along with my scoring average and, prior to the NBA Draft, I worked out for more than half of the top 26 teams. On Draft night, I eagerly awaited the call that I hoped would come. The family was all together watching the Draft on TV. With the Heat on the clock at #15, I excused myself from the room. Miami had not been one of the teams that worked me out so surely they wouldn't be drafting me. The buffet that we had set up for the night was calling from the next room, and now was the perfect time to answer. Moments later, the living room erupted in applause and joy. The Heat had drafted me!

In a few minutes, my agent called to tell me the whole story. He said, "Dave, you won't be playing for the Heat. They plan to ship you and Carl Herrera to the Houston Rockets in exchange for the Rockets' #12 pick, Alec Kessler."

Well, that made sense. I had a great workout for the Rockets, and I really liked them and felt comfortable there. That team, with Hakeem Olajuwon, Kenny Smith, Vernon Maxwell, et al, would eventually win the NBA Championship in 1994 and 1995. My life could not have been better, but still I felt something was missing.

My first season, 1990-91, went well. We made the playoffs and Don Chaney, our coach, was named Coach of the Year.

I hung out a lot that year with another rookie, David Wood. I got to spend a lot of time with him, and I noticed that there was something very different about him. I was not handling the pressures very well of being a young NBA player with money, traveling from one city to the next. A friend of mine compared what I was going through to trying to crush a Coke can. If it's full, it's hard to crush; if it's empty, it's easy.

I was empty and very crushable.

David, on the other hand, was strong and settled and content. Even joyful. I wondered what was going on with him, and eventually the conversations and dialogue started.

What I found was that he had a relationship with Jesus Christ. I did not. I was not opposed to Christianity or religion; I just had never been around it enough to know what it all meant. One evening, David invited me out for pizza, and he said, "You know, Dave, you don't have this relationship with Christ, and you can have it. If you'd be interested in knowing more, I have a pastor friend who would be happy to talk with you about it." I was and still am grateful that David cared enough about me to speak up and start a conversation that would literally change my life forever.

I did accept Christ, and almost immediately I began to hunger to know more about Him in every way. I played for the Rockets for a couple more years, and was on the last team before they won the NBA championship in 1994. I am thankful for that time, but I am even more thankful that it allowed me to meet David Wood, and most importantly, my Savior.

Today, I am a pastor at Renovate Church in Austin, Texas. I am exactly where I am supposed to be, and I love what I do. There was a time when I couldn't imagine loving anything more than basketball. I was wrong. My work is not work at all; it's a calling. I see lives changed just like mine, and it's a privilege. I am married to an amazing woman, April, and I have four wonderful children: Bret, Elijah, Trey and Mia. My heart is full, and my life is rich. I couldn't ask for more, really.

WAVING A WAND

I was asked an interesting question recently that gave me pause: If I could wave a wand over fatherhood in America, what one thing would I change?

Here's the truth: A big part of being the kind of father who lifts up his kids and makes them what they were meant to be is just being there, being present. I think back to what my father did for me. He was always there, and he wanted to hang out and spend time together. In fact, *he initiated it.* He would come to me in the afternoons after a long workday or on weekends when he could have just rested, and we went out and played basketball at open gyms and parks in the area where there was great competition.

That sounds simple when you say it like that, doesn't it? But here's what came from that. Think for a minute about this progression: My dad said I could play in the NBA, and I did. He spent time with me. He – like Jesus – said, "Come with me," and he planted the truth way down deep in my soul every time we got out on the court that it was not only doable, but sort of inevitable. I believed him, and he was right.

That alone would be pretty cool, wouldn't it? But then, because I played NBA basketball, I met a guy who led me to the biggest and most important decision I will ever make in this life: To become a Believer, to turn my life and my issues over to the One who has all the answers.

Real discipleship, like real fatherhood, is like that. It spurs people on to be their best, and gives them the tools and belief they'll need to accomplish it.

And, the great thing is, every father can do this. And when they do, I'm here to tell you, anything is possible.

——

ABOUT DAVE JAMERSON

Dave, a 2015 inductee into the Ohio Basketball Hall of Fame, played with the Houston Rockets, Utah Jazz and New Jersey Nets in the NBA after a record-breaking collegiate career. He then served as the President and International Director of Champions for Christ, was the founder and President of Champions Academy – a world-class basketball training academy that uses sports to reach and influence the next generation of basketball leaders – and served on the National Association of Basketball Coaches ministry team in charge of all outreach activities at the NCAA Final Four and Convention. Throughout his career, Dave has helped to plant churches and lead ministry in more than 30 countries. Today, Dave is the Lead Pastor of Renovate Church in Austin, Texas, and resides with his wife of 25 years, April, and their four children in Leander, Texas.

3 HE REALLY DOES LOVE YOU

By Jamey Codding
Marketing & Communications Manager, Christian Children's Home of Ohio

"But as for me and my house, we will serve the LORD."
Joshua 24:15 ESV

I AM in kindergarten. I am too young to understand divorce, but I know that I never see my dad and that the man who just married my mom kind of scares me. The wild beard that covers half of his face doesn't help, nor does his deafening motorcycle.

My mom tells me my new stepdad loves me. "He just has a hard time showing it." I end up hearing this a lot growing up. He teaches me how to ride a bike in a gravel parking lot. After countless falls and subsequent commands to "get back up," my knees and elbows are caked with blood, my face streaked with dust and tears. But, when we head home that afternoon, I am able to ride a bike.

He says, "I need to toughen you up." I'm not sure what that means but he says it a lot when I'm crying. He tells me about fights that he's been in, both as a kid and an adult. I secretly hope that I never get into a fight of my own.

He watches "Star Trek" every week. I watch it with him and memorize each word of the title sequence, but I think it's the dumbest show on TV. It's the first of many interests of his that I willfully reject. I prefer watching baseball instead, looking for faces I recognize from my growing collection of trading cards.

My mom sometimes talks to me about God. I believe that something created me and is up there somewhere, but I have no idea who it is or what that really means. We never go to church and I couldn't tell you if we own a Bible.

I AM in third grade. I miss my dad and wonder why he doesn't love me enough to see me more often or even send a birthday card. My mom says his Army job keeps him busy and makes it impossible for him to live closer to me.

He visits a couple times a year and I treasure each chance I have to spend time with him. He wears boots while playing basketball with me in the driveway. He says he lets me win but I know better. We go to the store and pick up the Ken Griffey Jr. rookie card I've wanted for months. He takes me for rides on his motorcycle. I think his bike is way cooler than my stepdad's.

I hate when his visits end and I'm left to return to my normal life. I want to live with my dad because there aren't any rules or restrictions when I'm with him, but I know my mom would never allow it. She and my stepdad argue more and more. It's worse when he drinks. Bernie Kosar, Ozzie Newsome and Hanford Dixon provide the perfect distraction.

I choose the Browns when I play friends in "Tecmo Super Bowl" and I know the words to all the silly fan songs played on WMMS. My favorite is "Bernie, Bernie." Like everyone else in northeast Ohio, I am convinced the Browns are headed to the Super Bowl. Instead, John Elway crushes those dreams during the 1987 AFC Championship Game as he marches down the field for the winning score late in the fourth quarter. A year later, our Super Bowl hopes are stripped from Earnest Byner's hands on the one-yard line against Elway's Broncos. I had no idea "The Drive" and "The Fumble" would be just the first of my Cleveland sports wounds.

I AM in sixth grade. I occasionally wonder if I would have the courage to commit suicide. I run away from home instead, away from my stepdad and all his rules and punishments. My friends find me deep in the woods at the back of our neighborhood and rat me out to my mom. I'm back home before sunset.

There are moments where my stepdad and I get along great. He takes me to the Richfield Coliseum for the first time, where I hear the name "World B. Freeeeeeeeeee" echo throughout the building. I later idolize Mark Price, but when Michael Jordan sinks "The Shot" over Craig Ehlo, I wonder if rooting for sports teams is supposed to be this painful. We go to several Indians games every year and I don't care that they stink. Cory Snyder and Joe Carter become my favorite players. Once, we even get Reggie Jackson to sign my mitt when the Oakland A's are in town. At a ballgame, playing catch in the front yard, shooting hoops in the driveway, wrestling in the living room – life is good in these moments.

But these moments rarely last long. My stepdad's patience is fleeting, his temper explosive. He never hits me, but intimidation is his parenting tool of choice. The threat of violence is very real. He smashes my "Donkey Kong" mini arcade game into a hundred pieces one day as punishment for...I don't remember.

I've grown tired of hearing my mom say, "He really does love you." Most days, I'm not even convinced that he likes me all that much. I'm unaware of the scars he carries from his own broken relationship with his father and the inner battles he fights each day because of them. All I see is a guy who isn't my dad telling me what to do and pointing out all the ways I screw up.

I AM in middle school. My dad writes to tell me he has a disease. I'm terrified but my mom tells me alcoholism isn't the kind of disease I think it is. Now I'm scared and confused. Only later would I realize both fathers in my life are alcoholics and neither seems all that interested in overcoming their addiction.

After being stationed in Germany and then on a small island near Hawaii, my dad takes a desk job with the Army one state away. He comes to watch a couple of my baseball and soccer games for the first time. Even better, he picks me up to spend one week each summer with him.

The magazines on the floor beside his bed grab my attention. Looking at the girls on the pages who aren't wearing any clothes makes me feel funny. I tear out some of the pictures. Later that night, my dad sits down next to me while I'm playing Nintendo and asks if there's anything I want to talk about, any questions I'd like to ask him. I say "no" without looking away from the screen and am relieved that our conversation ends there. I take the pictures home with me and find myself looking at the girls in my school differently.

When home life is particularly rough, I sometimes ask God for help, hoping to hear an answer. The ensuing silence tells me He either isn't listening or isn't there. I eventually stop asking.

I AM in high school. My dad drives in to watch some of my cross country and track races. He is there during my freshman year when I help our varsity team qualify for Regionals. He seems genuinely proud of me. I soak it in.

My stepdad teaches me how to drive stick and works with me for hours on my jump shot. He also drunkenly ridicules me in front of his friends at our Fourth of July cookout for not being "man enough." The moments with Dr. Jekyll don't erase the damage inflicted by Mr. Hyde. I spend as little time as possible at home and can't wait to escape to college.

My truck is zipping along an empty country road well above the speed limit when a woman pulls out of her driveway in front of me. She seems genuinely surprised to see me barreling toward her at 65 mph. Our wide eyes lock, horrified, just moments before the front of my truck would plow into her door. She slams on her brakes, her car stopping in my lane. We are both going to die. Instead, she hits the gas again and I swerve around her. Part of me believes that God just saved my life and part just dismisses it as dumb luck. I know which part I want to believe but I don't know why.

Nobody in our school or in my life ever talks about God or the importance of purity. Lots of people talk about sex. I have one goal: lose my virginity before graduation. I succeed. Several guys in our school become fathers before graduation. I'm fortunate to not be one of them.

I attend church once or twice a year with my new girlfriend's family and am uncomfortable through every minute of it. I don't know when to stand or when to sit or what to say; surely they are all watching me. Is the service almost over? I just want to open Christmas presents or eat Easter candy.

I am certain the Bible is a work of fiction but I want people to think I'm a "good guy," so I maintain my attendance with the C&E crowd. The Gospel? Never heard of it.

I AM a college freshman. My mom and stepdad both cry when they drop me off at my dorm. He tells me that he loves me and that I'm a good man. I'm stunned and don't know how to respond. It isn't the first time we hug, but this one is different. They drive away and I feel free. Finally. No friends to rat me out to my mom this time.

The Ohio University campus is filled with kids just like me. I am consumed with pride and selfishness and greed and lust. My mission is to make college "the best years of my life" but rather than trying to define what that actually means, I allow everyone else to define it for me.

I nearly flunk out before learning just how much studying I need to mix in with my partying to skate by. The world has sunk its hooks deep into me but I am blissfully ignorant. Instant gratification is my daily pursuit and I make one decision after another that begin to haunt me, chasing acceptance and everything else culture tells me I deserve while numbing the pain that inevitably follows.

I AM a junior in college. My temper is a sight to behold. After Tribe closer Jose Mesa blows a save in Game 7 of the 1997 World Series and the Marlins win the series two innings later, I walk down the hallway of our apartment complex in a fit of rage, smashing the light fixtures along the way. They explode just like my "Donkey Kong" game once did. Later that year, my roommates and I make threatening prank phone calls to random numbers on campus. We think they are hilarious. The people we called do not. Neither do the police.

We get drunk five or six nights a week. I start smoking marijuana too. Why not? Anything and everything goes in college. I am surrounded by friends and yet somehow feel alone, wondering when everyone will realize that I'm a fraud and abandon me.

I visit my dad each summer. He has a new wife and I have a new kid brother. The magazines are now hidden at the bottom of a stack of other reading material in the bathroom. I wonder how long it will take my brother to find them as I flip through the pages.

My stepdad and I get along much better when I come home to visit throughout the school year. The summer is a different story. After being on my own for nine months a year, I refuse to take orders from him for the other three.

He drinks more now that he's lost his job. I drink with him when I am home. He tries his hand at several other career paths but nothing pans out. Depression saturates his life and the fighting with my mom worsens. Their marriage is poisoned.

I AM a new college graduate on my own in a big city. I hate my first job and already dread the idea of working the rest of my life. My days feel hollow and insignificant. Is this what being an adult is all about? Again, I learn how to skate by, more interested in where we will party that night than in doing my job well. I drink almost as much as I did in college.

My past quietly torments me. Depression sets in. Without anyone in my life whose opinion I trust, I continue pursuing my warped concept of happiness while wondering what it really means to be a man. I have a nice car, a steady job, a huge apartment with several friends and an engagement ring on my fiancée's finger, yet none of it washes away the pain that has been germinating inside of me for years. Each day brings new choices that add to my suffering. I assume this is normal.

I AM newly married. This will finally make me happy.
Why isn't this making me happy?

I AM a new dad. This will finally make me happy.
Why am I even unhappier now?

Determined to get right everything my dad and stepdad got wrong, I focus on the kind of father I don't want to be rather than exploring the kind of father I want to become. I end up learning just how much like my stepdad I now am. My impatience and short fuse mirror his. I hate myself for it. I feel like I already am letting down my beautiful baby daughter, convinced that I don't deserve to be her dad.

I don't know how to be myself with my wife because I don't know which version of me is the real one. Mandy thinks I am one way; her family thinks I am another; my family, another; my friends, another one still. Yet nobody knows my despair, and I don't recognize the guilt that threatens to consume my family.

I now have a son. I am drowning. Mandy and the kids deserve someone so much better than me. Will I ever figure life out? Is happiness a myth? I thought adults were supposed to have life all figured out. Are we all just privately miserable behind our lying, smiling faces? I dutifully uphold the charade while secretly dreading the day when everyone sees the real me. I search for answers in new age and self-help books, but I find smoking pot is the only way to escape my bleak reality.

My son Andrew is timid and sensitive. This annoys me. I frighten him, which annoys me more. It seems clear that I need to toughen him up. For his sake. The irony is lost on me. Against all odds, Emma has become "Daddy's Little Girl" but Andrew seemingly wants nothing to do with me.

With no support from me, my wife's faith is withering. She seeks out a church to attend with the kids. I occasionally tag along during her church hunting, mostly to reinforce my belief that religion is a sham. When our second son is born, Mandy's search intensifies. My depression deepens.

I ask the pastor who will christen Eliot my most loaded questions about faith. He smiles and listens, politely answering each one. At the end of our conversation, he boils the Christian faith down to one essential question: Do you believe that Jesus died and rose from the grave? It sounds like a bad soap opera storyline. Moving along, nothing to see here.

My mom and stepdad's marriage is over. The divorce hits me much harder than expected. She begins to find healing, but he spirals out of control. My relationship with him fractures further.

I AM 35. Life is pointless. I work from home and keep myself isolated from my family most nights, pretending to work. Now stuck in the middle of my mom and stepdad's divorce, I find myself resenting both of them. I don't remember the last time I've spoken to my dad, much less seen him, and at this point I don't really care. I'm tired of trying. I do my best as a dad myself but I know it's not nearly good enough for my three young kids.

Months after becoming friends with someone from my neighborhood, I learn he is a pastor at Freshwater Community Church. Horrified, I wonder, "How many times have I sworn in front of Steve?" Over time, I share with him my views on faith and religion, but I am not as confident in them as I once was. He too smiles and listens. Soon, I find myself sitting next to Mandy in Steve's church. I am skeptical yet, somehow, hopeful. Could the answers I desperately need be found in the one place I so forcefully rejected?

The worship music stirs something up inside of me. The lyrics on the screen at the front of the room – hopeful words that speak to the pain I feel and point toward a truth that I was sure did not exist – begin to swim as unexpected tears fill my eyes. The pastor that day may as well be talking directly to me, his message identifying wounds I'd carried for years. My heart simultaneously aches and leaps with anticipation. I can't comprehend what's happening but I don't want it to end. I later learn that the presence of God met me in that sanctuary. I want more.

"You know that God loves you unconditionally, right?" I'm not really sure what Steve means. Over time, I would come to realize that, in response to feeling rejected by my dad and stepdad, I concluded that the amount I was loved directly corresponded to the amount of good I had done, so I needed to work harder to earn my worth. But as my mistakes in life began piling up, I considered myself to be unworthy of love. Even from my own wife and kids.

Steve explains the Gospel, that even what I believe to be unforgiveable mistakes can be forgiven because Jesus willingly died on the cross as punishment for each of my sins. Terrified but finally hopeful, I confess my deepest, darkest sins to a God I don't yet know but can no longer deny. I'm crying yet again.

In the days, weeks and months that follow, true joy and peace enter my heart. The clouds of depression break and, after smoking pot to escape my hopeless reality for nearly 10 years, God completely removes that debilitating crutch from my life. He leads me to confess to the people I've hurt most, and I watch Jesus restore and refine those damaged relationships. What once seemed impossible to me now stands as undeniable evidence that God is real, that Jesus can redeem all things, that the Spirit moves and works in miraculous ways.

I apologize to my stepdad for the resentment and hostility I harbored for so long, and I forgive him for the mistakes he made when I was a kid and for letting alcohol destroy his marriage to my mom. I also thank him for purposefully filling the gap my dad had vacated. My stepdad wasn't perfect but he was there, and he tried to give me what he thought I needed.

He starts attending Freshwater with us and seems genuinely interested in pursuing a deeper understanding of who God is. He also joins AA and begins collecting a regular paycheck again. Unfortunately, happiness and sobriety prove to be elusive. We talk often about finding joy and purpose in his current life situation instead of dwelling on mistakes that can't be undone, but I know that is deep, soul-changing work that only God can accomplish. My stepdad is stubborn but so was I. Our God, meanwhile, is patient and powerful.

I also apologize to my dad for my part in abandoning our relationship as an adult. I forgive him for the times he failed to show up, to be present, to make an effort. We talk things through shortly after my grandfather passes away and agree to work toward repairing our relationship. The initial progress is slow but I trust in God's timing and continue praying for healing.

For years, I yearned for guidance, for loving correction and invaluable lessons that would equip me to deal with the pain this world mercilessly doles out. I now know that these things come from my Heavenly Father, that despite the shortcomings of my earthly fathers, our God never fails. And when I look back on my own struggles as a man, husband and father who wandered aimlessly without the Lord, I'm grateful that grace and forgiveness have flooded areas of my life where previously there was only bitterness and pain. I know all too well that life can deeply wound anyone, and those wounds are bound to bleed onto the people closest to us.

My wife and children suffered collateral damage as I wrestled through years of my empty existence. After being saved, I apologize to Mandy for the isolation and self-medication. We commit our marriage to God and lay our family at His feet, praying for guidance as we seek to honor Him and encourage each other through trials and triumphs alike. With the counsel of our pastors and trusted friends, we watch God strengthen our marriage and our friendship in miraculous ways.

I now have men in my life that I respect, husbands and fathers who point me toward God's design for marriage and family, who help me embrace my responsibility to these three remarkable kids. My family tree has forever been changed. I know I'm going to mess up, I know I won't have all the answers, but I also know that's okay. I've been entrusted with a sacred duty to prepare them for a world that desperately needs their light and love to shine bright, to illuminate its darkest corners. After feeling unworthy of this calling for so long, I now thank God for such an incredible opportunity.

However, I still have trouble relating to my oldest son. Andrew and I find some common interests with video games and Legos and "Star Wars," but he prefers to keep me at arm's length and shows absolutely no interest in watching the Cleveland sports teams that have been such a big part of my life. I continue praying for a breakthrough while silently worrying that we will never enjoy the close relationship I envisioned having with my kids.

I AM a LeBron James fan again. Andrew begins asking questions about LeBron after he returns to Cleveland in 2014. All of my kids start watching the Cavs games with Mandy and me. A year later, Andrew plays organized basketball for the first time. It's love at first sight. During Andrew's practices, I shoot hoops with Eliot on the other side of the court. He pretends to be LeBron, then Kevin Love, then J.R. Smith. He tells me he wants to play next season too.

It's playoff time. After getting knocked out of the Finals the previous season by Steph Curry's Warriors, we are excited for the Cavs to get another chance at them. The kids stay up late each night of the Finals, asking question after question on the couch next to me. They are tired the next morning but my wife and I know opportunities like this don't come often, at least not in Cleveland. We hope their memories are better than "The Fumble" and "The Shot."

After we all enjoy a Father's Day breakfast together, Emma and Andrew leave for summer Bible camp, hours before Game 7 of the Finals tips off. Fortunately, they will get to watch the game with the other kids and their counselors. Mandy, Eliot and I watch from our living room. I wish we were all together, but I am grateful they will get to experience a night like this.

"Why are you standing up, Dad?" It's just after halftime. I tell Eliot that I can't sit. Neither can Mandy. "The Block." "The (New) Shot." Love's defensive stop. Is this really going to happen? Time ticks down. A missed three from the corner. Ballgame. Jumping up and down. Tears. Hugs. Utter disbelief. Eliot runs around the room, screaming. He may not know the history, the torture from the past 52 years, but he soaks in the moment as only a seven year old can.

When Emma and Andrew are back home, we all watch replays of the game together and rewind to see the most crucial plays over and over. My boys now want to collect basketball cards. I show them the thousands upon thousands of baseball cards I have in a crate in the basement. The Ken Griffey Jr. rookie that my dad bought me nearly 30 years ago sits among them. I take the boys to the local card shop. Andrew picks out a Channing Frye and Eliot snags a K-Love – their favorite Cavs players. Together we pore over the hundreds of cards they get in the commons packs and put the best ones in binders and protective cases. They spend hours sorting through their collections and making countless trades.

Just as LeBron's return ignited an interest in the Cavaliers, the Indians' run atop the standings has my boys following Frankie Lindor, Jason Kipnis and Corey Kluber all summer. They play baseball in the front yard and shoot hoops in the alley, coming home each day with dirty faces and scabbed knees. Seemingly overnight, they have become sports nuts and love the Cavs and Tribe as much as I did when I was their age. They even now follow the Browns, for better or worse, and they clearly believe I'm some sort of sports Siri, peppering me with random questions that even Google would have to Google.

I AM riding a train with Mandy and the kids to downtown Cleveland. It's warmer than expected on this October evening and there is barely enough room to stand among the crowd of fans wearing Cavs and Tribe gear for what promises to be one of the most memorable nights in Cleveland sports history.

We exit the train and walk through Tower City, Mandy and I doing our best to keep the kids close in the chaos. We spill out onto Ontario Avenue with thousands of other people and can already hear the buzz from down the street. ESPN has a crew on site. So do TNT and all the local news stations.

It's Ring Night for the Cavaliers as LeBron, Kyrie and the rest of their teammates open the season against the New York Knicks after watching the team's first championship banner get raised into the rafters. My family and I, meanwhile, will be next door in Progressive Field for Game 1 of the World Series against the Chicago Cubs.

A night like this would have seemed impossible not that long ago, but this is New Cleveland, Title Town, Believeland. Mandy, the kids and I take pictures in front of a backdrop of the Larry O'Brien trophy as we soak in the incredible atmosphere between Quicken Loans Arena and Progressive Field. Eliot informs me that this is his first World Series game. Join the club.

I savor the joy I feel sharing this night with the four people I love most, experiencing a moment that we won't ever forget. Among a sea of giddy Cavs and Indians fans who are celebrating the past and looking toward the future, I praise God for the work He has done in my life, the ways His Spirit has forever changed me, the healing He has blessed my family with and the path along which He now leads us. I smile as I reflect on how He used sports to bring us closer together, even bridging a gap between Andrew and me that once seemed too cavernous to cross.

Yet I also recognize that my kids need more from me. Sports matter but rarely as much as we think. These games have an incredibly unique way of creating bonds between people – family members and strangers alike – but we often allow sports to sit a little too high on our list of priorities. So while I'm thankful that my Cleveland sports heritage has been passed down to my kids, it's much more important to pass my faith down and encourage them to make it their own.

We scream our heads off that night as Kluber and unlikely hero Roberto Perez lead the home team to a convincing 6-0 win. The next morning, we call the kids off school, sleep in, and then flip on the DVR to watch the Cavs spank the Knicks 117-88 in our pajamas. Memories don't get much more perfect than that.

But just a week later, the Indians' season concludes with an ending seemingly torn from the pages of Old Cleveland's history books, losing Game 7 at home in extra innings after owning a 3-1 series lead. It's my kids' first heartbreaking "Moment" – this one may go down as "The Rain Delay." (Ask Siri if you don't know why.)

But there are no shattered light fixtures for me this night. It's a disappointing finale, to be sure, but even more so, it's a reminder that my identity isn't tied to whether or not my favorite team scores more runs, makes more baskets or reaches the end zone more often than its opponent. Win or lose, I am still blessed beyond my wildest dreams because my joy is not found in the numbers on a scoreboard, nor is it dictated by past mistakes or even the relationships with the people in my life.

I finally found true joy and peace when a gracious and loving God redeemed my broken vision of fatherhood. He sacrificed everything to be with me, and now I need to point my kids toward their perfect Father while following His example and being transparent with them about my faults and failures.

I will let them down. He never will.

_____

ABOUT JAMEY CODDING

After Jamey spent 35 years with both feet firmly planted in the world, the experience of having God completely turn his life upside down has been both thrilling and terrifying. He is honored to play a small part in the incredible work being done by CCHO and its family of ministries, but even more grateful for the people he gets to come home to each night. He enjoys good food, good music, good TV and good coffee, and he is always in search of more time to read, write and take pictures. Most of all, he loves running with Emma, playing ping pong with Andrew, shooting hoops with Eliot and watching his teams with his family, but his favorite pastime has to be holding his wife's hand.

4 CAMI COMES HOME

By Ron Rodak

President, ASAP, Advertising Specialties and Printing, LLC in North Canton, OH

"See what kind of love the Father has given to us,

that we should be called children of God; and so we are."

1 John 3:1 ESV

My wife and I raised our family in northeast Ohio and, of course, we are all avid Browns, Indians and Cavs fans. With two sons and a daughter, we had lots of outings as a family to Cleveland sporting events. We have collected sports cards and bought mountains of team memorabilia, from shirts and hats to pennants and cups.

Unfortunately, our relationship with these teams had long been defined by two words: "So close." The Browns came "so close" in the '80s, and the '97 Indians nearly gave us a World Series title, but both teams ultimately fell just short. But then came LeBron James and the Cavaliers in the 2016 NBA Finals.

Down 3-1, a deficit no NBA team had previously overcome in the Finals, the Cavs needed a miracle to secure the city's first championship since forever ago. Little did I know, but God had a real Father's Day Miracle in store for our family.

Game 6, on 6-16-16. A must-win night in a hostile opponent's arena thousands of miles away from their loyal Cleveland fans. The Cavs had to perform! No one expected them to win. Another season lost. Another Cleveland team getting "so close" only to come up empty.

Or could they somehow pull it off? Surely, Cleveland fans would not be disappointed again. AHHH...such drama!

But the drama wasn't just in the game. My daughter had been in labor for hours as tipoff approached, and there was no progress. My wife and I had been in Charlestown, SC for more than a week waiting for this momentous occasion – our grandchild's birth, not Game 6.

And there was no TV in the waiting room.

Okay, don't panic – I have my phone and can stream the game. Wait – no cell phone reception either!

The rest of the evening, I admit, was kind of a blur but I'll do my best to describe what all happened.

I certainly could not make a big deal about the TV. (Oh, woe is me!) Of course, my wife knew I cared for my daughter and that I would not leave the waiting room unless given permission from her (without ever really asking for permission) to go watch the game until the arrival of the real miracle – not a Cleveland win; the baby, my first grandchild, my only granddaughter.

So after my wife told me to go find a TV, I tracked one down and watched the game for five minutes before she called me back to the room: the baby was coming.

Moments later, the miracle happened. (I didn't know about the Cavs yet.) Camilla Grace, born 6-16-16 on the night of Game 6. Suddenly, I wasn't nervous at all about the outcome of the game. Instead, I was overjoyed with the new life in my arms and overcome by a love that only a father (and now grandfather) could feel for their children (and this beautiful granddaughter).

We took Camilla home three nights later to watch her first Cavs game: NBA Finals, Game 7. We were not thinking about the miracle that was about to happen across the country in Oakland. We were thinking about the blessing of life that God had given our family.

Cami, our little dear one, is truly a miracle, one that was waited on patiently and prayerfully and faithfully by her parents for many years. She was a Game

6 Miracle in advance of not only a Father's Day Homecoming full of answered prayers for our family, but also a Father's Day Miracle that represented an answer to decades of prayers for Cleveland fans.

———

ABOUT RON RODAK

Follower of Christ, Husband 4Life #truelove, Father of Three #4Ever, and a GrandPops #4EverMore! Building Christ followers for eternity and a NE Ohio sports family fan base for generations to come, one at a time!

5 WALT AND DEE AND A STREET PARTY

By Steve Doerschuk
Cleveland Browns writer, *The Canton Repository*

"Honor your father and your mother, that your days may be
long in the land that the Lord your God is giving you."
Exodus 20:12 ESV

My two cents on the Father's Day Miracle has something to do with LeBron, sure, but it really goes back to the old Cleveland Arena. Trust me when I tell you, 7,000 people in that place could sound like the loudest 21,000 you have ever heard in "The Q."

I was in high school when the Cavaliers were born, and I didn't care how bad they were as a start-up expansion team. It was love at first sight, and it was the same with my best friends. They weren't a third as good as the LeBron James teams, but they had three times as many players we recognized without using their surnames. Bingo. Foots. A.C.

Some of those friends were my teammates on a basketball team at Westbrook Park United Methodist Church. The coach was Benny Griffiths, then and now one of the best men I have known. You may never meet him on this side, but ask for him when you get to heaven. He will be there, and he will be glad to meet you.

Anyway, Benny arranged a trip to the Arena during the Cavs' second year. The opponent was the New York Knicks, who were fantastic then, with a roster including Earl "The Pearl" Monroe and Jerry Lucas. Our seats were at the top of the Arena. The tickets probably cost five bucks, but we had as much fun at that game as any we have ever attended.

The Cavs weren't supposed to have a chance, but they were really scrappy and they hung around. When a guard named Butch Beard made a steal and a dunk to send the Cavs to a win, my friends and I were standing on our wooden seats, delirious. But then, all 7,000 people in the Arena were going nuts.

I was never cured. The Cavs have been my team ever since, and they still are, two arenas later.

That is the NBA side of my Father's Day Miracle tale.

For me, though, the Father's Day Miracle must be told in the context of the very best man I ever met. Sure, I'm biased. It was my dad.

And I'm saying this four decades after he died on the day after Christmas.

Dad remains very real to me. Here's some of who he was.

Walter Doerschuk was born 30 years after basketball was invented. He grew up near what is now Skyland Pines Rustic Lodge, where I have covered many sports banquets in a long career as a newspaper writer. For a long time now, I have covered the Browns for the *Canton Repository*.

One definition of rustic is "made of rough wood." Here's a detailed definition of rough:

Dad was one of 12 brothers and sisters. One sister got hit by a car and died, which would be enough to rock any family's world. When their father died, it was worse.

Dad's father, also a Walter, was a carpenter. I have always supposed he worked himself to death. All I know for sure is that Dad's mom, Jesse, was pregnant with her 12th child, Ruth, when the original Walter was working in the hot sun and collapsed.

I wonder about the grandpa I never met. He didn't live to see the Great Depression.

The family soldiered on without a father through the thick of the Depression. Here's the short form of what the Depression meant for millions of Americans, including the Doerschuks: tomato sandwiches for dinner when there was nothing else. Often enough, there was nothing but each other. In an age of staring at cell phones, it's a lesson that can go a long way.

But there was faith. I can't imagine how my relatives could have made it without a faith that has been imparted to their children and their children's children. My uncle George is the lone survivor among the 12 siblings. Jesus has been prominent in all 11 of the funerals.

What happened after all those children lost their father could fill a book. The Doerschuks found an old farmhouse in Canton Township. The kids did subsistence farming. The oldest brother, Ray, got a 37-cents-an-hour factory job. Their mother, my grandma, was a rock.

I did get to know my widowed grandmother, from a little boy's perspective. She was full of serenity and patience. Maybe she was too tired to yell at us while we ran roughshod through the house where she lived alone after all the kids moved out.

Grandma died in 1964, the year the Browns won a National Football League championship.

Dad and George survived a "business trip" to the South Pacific and together opened an auto repair shop on Sherman Church Road after World War II. George married shortly after the war. His wife, Dorothy, worked with a young woman named Delores Lehmann. Walt and Delores's first date was with George and Dorothy. It was supposed to include an Indians game, but they never made it to the stadium. Walt got pulled over for speeding in Cleveland and was taken to jail. Long story short: Everything got worked out that night. What a first date, though. I am lucky to be writing this.

Walt and Delores (everyone called her Dee) married and had four sons. We grew up on 50 acres in Canton Township — the land where all of those siblings moved after their dad died. Mom was a very smart lady. She taught me grammar and forced me to pick a school activity other than sports. I picked the school newspaper.

Maybe I got my love for the Indians from Dee as well. Everybody knew about Indian greats Bob Feller and Lou Boudreau, but it was Mom who told me about the lesser lights. I learned of Roy "Stormy" Weatherly, a colorful centerfielder who stood just 5-foot-6, only through her.

Mom and Dad got married in 1950, the year the Browns jumped to the NFL. The sons came along in (sports drop-in included) 1952 (Browns reach NFL title game), 1954 (Tribe wins 111 games), 1955 (Otto Graham goes out with an NFL title) and 1964 (Browns beat Johnny Unitas to win it all).

The big winning in Cleveland stopped after 1964.

Dad could talk about anything, and he made many friends, but he didn't have time to be a sports nut.

He ran his gas station after George struck out on his own. He farmed the 50 acres, near a country school – Prairie College – where Ralph Regula was the principal before he was a congressman. He and Mom had an active social and church life, making time to be good friends and neighbors. They put together corn roasts in the side yard and square dances in the barn.

I can't imagine being as busy as Dad was. It went beyond the necessary hard-knocks education of surviving the Depression. He was an industrious, optimistic, dry-witted, good-hearted man of God.

I don't mean to slight Mom in any of this. She was the best mom in the world.

Dad made time for sports. At least, he made time to make sure that we could enjoy them. He dug out some ground near our creek. He and his friends turned it into the pond where we played hockey in January. These same people built a baseball field where all of my friends hung out in July.

Dad had an unorthodox bowling delivery that made people laugh. He was stocky and strong, and the ball would fly for a while after he let it go, landing with a thud. His average wasn't great, something like 10, but he made the pins explode.

One of his clients was Spring Valley golf course, where he maintained the engine that powered the irrigation system. We got a family membership in exchange for his work. Some Sundays before church, he would drive us to Spring Valley. We would tee off before sunrise, hitting balls into mist. You couldn't find your ball until you located the trail in the dew.

I grew up loving all the sports. I loved playing every one. I knew all the players and all the stats. One of my brothers kept a Browns scrapbook. I kept an Indians scrapbook. All of us played baseball on what is now Walter Doerschuk Field, and basketball on the hoop he put up in the driveway on Sherman Church Road.

Dad wanted us to have more fun that it was possible for him to have had as a kid.

Mom and Dad both died in the 1970s. Having them as parents, if only for barely more than 20 years, was a blessing I can't begin to describe. I should have done more for them. I would encourage anyone to do more for your parents than you think you have time for.

Fortunately, as I have mentioned, there is faith. There is Christianity. Through His grace, I have come to grips with my former regrets.

I have been blessed with eight children: five sons and three daughters. One of the daughters, Madison, didn't quite make it to this side, but I can tell you of a voice I heard one time while gazing at the shimmer on a bay. I was sure it was Madison's. The words were soft, wise, clear, overpowering: "It's all right."

Admittedly, this has been a circuitous route to the night of the Father's Day Miracle – the Cavaliers' victory against the Golden State Warriors, coming all the way back from being down three games to one. But I would ask you to understand. Some of these things I have not thought of for years, and I would not be thinking them now if I had not set out to write about that basketball event.

"The miracle" – Cleveland's first major sports championship since 1964 – was miraculous for reasons well known to people of my age and disposition.

The Indians wandered in the desert for many years and didn't even make it all the way out in 1997, when a ninth-inning lead in Miami turned into a Game 7 defeat. They didn't even make it out in 2016, when they were up three games to one on the Cubs.

The Browns barely missed Super Bowls in the 1980s, left us all numb by moving to Baltimore, and for the longest time have been a moonshot from winning.

The Cavaliers did not exist until 1970. Even though they are older than Marco Rubio, they had never won an NBA championship. Not when there was a "Miracle in Richfield." Not when Craig Ehlo should have used a pogo stick to guard Michael Jordan. Not in the early age of LeBron. Never, ever, going into the night of June 19, 2016.

It was a Sunday...Father's Day.

You may remember that night very well. Do you remember that day?

Whereas the temperature for an Indians World Series watch party plunged to about 40 on Oct. 30 in Progressive Field, it was too hot for charcoal on June 19. The temperature in Cleveland approached 90 degrees.

The anticipation for the game simmered all day. Our family started it at First Christian Church, which is where I met Joe Franz, a driving force behind this book. I was one of the dads who didn't have to be asked where I was going to spend Father's Day. It would lead to watching the Cavs playing in Oakland for the NBA title.

I looked forward to this perhaps even more than I savored the Indians' World Series games in the 1990s. This was true even though we would be watching the Cavs on TV, whereas I had attended all 13 of the Tribe's World Series games, home and away. It was part of my job with the *Repository*. It was pinch-me-so-I-know-it's-real work, getting paid to see the team of my youth in the World Series.

However, I have learned there is nothing like sharing a special moment with one's family, and no part of me wished I was in Oakland by myself to see the Cavs take on Golden State for Game 7. It was all about soaking it in with my wife, Sheila, the kids, and a few thousand of our closest friends.

My married daughters, Jackie and Margaret, wound up watching the game at their homes in Kirtland and Cincinnati. Sheila and our five sons (Jim, Walt, Rob, Noah, Zach) had a pleasant Father's Day doing I forget what, and then headed to a Canton sports bar to watch history.

The spot was Jerzee's, a drive and a 3-iron from the Pro Football Hall of Fame.

The atmosphere was rich and tense. Our older boys got plugged into rooting for the local pro teams years ago. The younger ones got hooked that night.

The Jerzee's parking lot was full, the bar was full, the eating tables were full, and the outdoor patio was full. The moon was full before the next morning, and most people saw it, because most people didn't go to bed that night.

The Warriors were heavy favorites, coming off a record-setting regular season, playing at home. The Cavs had been gritty throughout the series, though, and they hung tough in the first half.

The crowd at Jerzee's was fully invested before halftime, exuding a palpable group thought: "There's a chance."

As the game wore on, the howling for every Cavs basket got louder. Perhaps the beer did some of the talking, but mostly it was the inspiration of the moment, the team, the gathering of family, the reaching out to strangers, the "us."

It was also the geography, the "here." Our teams don't win championships. We stay with them for other reasons. We have been the underdogs who never win.

Yet, we press on. This is home, our most special place in the world, and these are our people.

The Warriors would not go away. Steph Curry's annoying mouthguard kept popping out, as if to taunt people who have only ever seen things go wrong in the end for their teams.

The Cavs would not go away. Our team was playing with skill and courage. We felt a part of it, as if our energy could roll across the land to California like some supercharged radio wave, with a face.

By the third quarter, I was no longer a 61-year-old man. I had turned back into a little boy. I knew I would be driving to Cleveland after the game, if the Cavs could pull it out. "Just to see what it was like, even though it would entail staying up long after midnight. I also knew the disposition of one of my sons well enough to know I only needed to mention this, and that his response would be, "I'm in."

We told everyone else in the family they were welcome to join us. They looked at us as if we had three heads.

But that was in the third quarter. By the time the fourth quarter was rolling, the mood had heightened.

The people at this table were giving high fives to the people at that table with every basket. The people on the patio were rolling like a wave. Eyes were wild and faces were lit.

People were having an effect on each other, and the sum of it was joy.

My family huddled at two tall round tables in the middle of it all. Sheila is full of tolerance and grace as to the sports in our house but has not been a sports fan per se. On this night, she was ready to stand on a wooden chair in the old Cleveland Arena.

"I didn't think it would be like this," she said as the game wound toward triple zeroes.

Our youngest son, 10-year-old Zach, normally doesn't last 10 minutes before losing interest in a game the rest of us are watching on TV. On this night, he couldn't get enough. As he watched the game, looked around at the people and gave his umpteenth high five to his brothers, his face really was equal to the description "lit up like a Christmas tree."

The game clock was one thing. The last half hour of real time was surreal. There was very little scoring but a lifetime of rising, falling and often agonizing in the air. This was prolonged during commercial breaks.

Time stood still between the late baskets. LeBron hit a three to put the Cavs up 89-87 with five minutes left. The Warriors tied it with a basket at 4:39, but no one scored again for the longest time.

When Kyrie Irving hit a three to give the Cavs a lead with 53 seconds left, Jerzee's was a wonderland. The impossible dream alit on the cusp of reality.

It became a moment frozen in time, sending chills when recalled. It was transcendent for our family in this sense: The unconvinced became convinced. When the championship was won, everyone wanted to make that spontaneous drive to Cleveland.

With 10 seconds left, LeBron went to the line. Just for old times, to make some poetry of the 50-plus years since a Cleveland team won a big-league sports championship, he missed the first foul shot to keep it a one-possession game.

The second shot went swish.

Time ran out. Time stands still.

These months later, Sheila gets this smile on her face when she remembers the boys jumping up and down as they hugged each other.

I did a lap around Jerzee's and found my way back to the family. It was a long way to Cleveland. Up we went. When we got there, sons and daughters of a million moms and dads were everywhere in sight, making music known only to this part of the sports world deep into the night.

It was like the song from the old "Drew Carey Show" echoing on and on: "Ohio, Ohio, Ohio."

Man, the street party was fun.

The time came to return to earth. The memory of the Father's Day Miracle remains.

Dad died the day after Christmas in 1976. I had never thought of it this way, but it occurs to me now. That was the year of the Cavs' "Miracle in Richfield."

We didn't have Mom much longer.

Both of them are very real to me to this day, in a life filled with far more blessings than I deserve.

If you know the Christian life, you hardly need me to tell you it is the only way to travel. As fellow travelers, we would agree, I think, that the Father's Day Miracle is a blessing to savor, not a grim punch line from an old Peggy Lee song: "Is that all there is?"

The Father's Day Miracle gives us pause to reflect on our best days here, sports and otherwise. Loved ones at our sides. Dear ones alive in our memories and spirits.

Speaking for one old sports dad, I would say the Father's Day Miracle inspired assorted happy thoughts.

Among them: Imagining the day I see Mom and Dad again.

––––

ABOUT STEVE DOERSCHUK
My mom made me join the school newspaper in 1970. A lot has happened since then. Long story short, I'm blessed in family and friends, and hopefully have developed an ear for what He wants out of me.

6 HARDWOOD LIFE LESSONS

By Kevin Hewitt
President & Chief Executive Officer, Christian Children's Home of Ohio

> *"By this my Father is glorified, that you bear much*
> *fruit and so prove to be my disciples."*
> John 15:8 ESV

When Marreese Speights' three try from the corner was not followed by a whistle indicating a possible four-point play and a subsequent tie ball game last Father's Day, I realized that our Cleveland Cavaliers were going to be NBA champions! I then needed to remind myself to breathe and to back away from the television set, perched above our fireplace. I had jumped off my familiar, comfortable couch when LeBron James chased down Andre Iguodala's layup and I had leapt closer when Kyrie Irving's three from the wing found nothing but net, but now I had to grasp the reality that the Cavs had done it, coming back from a three-games-to-one deficit!

As the buzzer sounded, my wife of 26 years, Lori, and I began yelling, hugging and dancing. After a couple moments of euphoria, we quieted enough to discuss the fact that one of our beloved Cleveland teams had won a championship. We were both struck by how cool it was that our city's first championship in 52 years was in basketball, a sport that has played an integral part of my life.

My first memory of basketball occurred in the third grade at Myers Elementary when a friend, Dave Burkett, brought in his basketball. Not to sound corny, but it was love at first sight: we played basketball every day at recess, and pretty soon I had convinced my mom and dad to put a hoop on our garage at home. This would prove to be the first of many: I had Nerf hoops and hoops made out of coffee cans scattered throughout our house and garage. I would play at school and then wait for my dad to get home from work so I could challenge him to a game. It wasn't until becoming a father myself that I fully appreciated the time my dad took to play ball with me.

My first Cavaliers memories are from this period as well. Lying in bed listening to Joe Tait describe the Cavs action on my little radio brings a smile to my face even today. From Bobby "Bingo" Smith, Austin Carr, Campy Russell, Jim Chones, Jim Cleamons, Phil Hubbard and Dick Snyder, all the Cavaliers became my heroes, and I faintly recall the 1976 "Miracle of Richfield" playoffs. My interest in sports, particularly basketball, had been ignited.

Junior high was my first real opportunity to play competitive basketball and we enjoyed championship seasons both years. It was the spring after our eighth grade season that I first met a coach who would have a tremendous impact on my life. Sitting in class one day, I was told that someone wanted to talk to me in the hall. I was surprised to find Coach Jim Kurzen waiting to speak to me; so surprised, in fact, that I don't think I even looked up at him as he talked to me. Coach Kurzen was somebody whom I deeply admired, having graduated from my school, Tuslaw, and then playing four years at Western Michigan University before ultimately getting to play in the NCAA tournament in 1976. Coach Kurzen asked if I would like to play ball that summer with the high school kids. Of course I said, "Yes."

Playing for Coach Kurzen that summer, I began to notice certain things about him, like his ability to maintain his composure regardless of the situation. The fall of my freshman year brought many exciting changes and challenges, including breaking my wrist playing dodgeball the day before my first freshman football game. Coach Kurzen also led the Fellowship of Christian Athletes (FCA) at Tuslaw. I have to admit that I may have gone to my first FCA meeting just to impress

Coach, but afterward I also began to have big questions about life, salvation and what happens when you die. Little did I know that in a couple of months, those questions would become immensely important to me, and it all started the weekend before my first official high school basketball practice.

REAL ANSWERS TO REAL QUESTIONS

My only sibling, Scot, was a junior that year and played on the Tuslaw football team. The last game of the year was against Lake, and Scot played defensive back for the varsity team Friday night before quarterbacking the junior varsity team Saturday morning. During the JV game, Scot was knocked unconscious while running the ball and was taken to the hospital. After several tests, a mass was discovered in Scot's abdomen and exploratory surgery was scheduled for Monday morning, the same day of my first high school basketball practice. I knew something was wrong when my neighbor's dad picked me up after practice instead of one of my parents. The neighbor told me that the exploratory surgery that was supposed to take 90 minutes ended up lasting more than seven hours. When my parents arrived home, they informed me that the surgeon had found a grapefruit-sized tumor in Scot's large intestine. The tumor turned out to be cancerous, and thus began an intensive period of treatment, including monthly chemotherapy trips to the National Institutes of Health. Scot lost his hair and had to wear a colostomy bag for several months.

With all the questions surrounding my brother's health, I found solace in basketball. For a couple of hours a day, in the gym, things were normal. I knew if I worked hard, I would get better. I didn't know if working hard would make Scot better. For the first time in my life, I was faced with end-of-life questions. What would happen to my brother if he didn't get better? What if he died? Coach Kurzen was there for me when I had questions. He clearly had a peace about these types of questions, telling me that Jesus Christ had conquered death when He rose again after being crucified. Coach explained that in Romans 6, Paul wrote that the wages of sin are death, but the gift of God is eternal life through Jesus Christ our God.

Even though Coach's words and the scriptures he suggested brought comfort, I still struggled to understand why a "good" person would need Jesus Christ's sacrifice. One day, I walked into the locker room with a question I was sure would stump Coach Kurzen and ease my conscience: "So you're telling me that if I am the best person in the world, if I give all my money to the needy, if I never lie and if I am nice to everyone, I still need to accept Jesus as my personal Lord and Savior?" Coach simply looked at me and answered, "Yes." I wasn't expecting that. I figured he would give a long, drawn out argument that I could attempt to reason away. Now I was faced with a decision: Either I could accept the free grace of Christ or continue to try to do things my way.

HIGH SCHOOL HIGHS

Scot successfully battled the cancer and was able to return to school after nearly a year's absence while I found myself diving headlong into sports, with basketball being my first love. I cannot pinpoint one single reason for my love of the game. I love its beauty – a well-run fast break where the ball is passed down the court teammate to teammate before being laid up off the glass and through the rim. I love its rhythm – the staccato sound of balls bouncing in the gym. I love the artistry of a no-look pass or a pure jump shooter's release of the ball off his fingertips, the perfect rotation of the ball before swishing through the basket. I love the strategy of the game, from drawing up a game-winning play to devising a defense to stop that all-world player. I love the physical aspect of basketball, the constant movement, pushing yourself harder and further than you ever thought you could, one last sprint to recover the loose ball on the baseline, saving it in to a teammate, jumping up and sprinting back down the court and receiving a return pass and then whipping a no-look bounce pass to a teammate cutting along the baseline for an uncontested layup. Oh, man, I think I may need to find a court before I finish writing this.

My high school basketball career had many ups and downs. Our Tuslaw team endured a 40-game losing streak, spanning the end of my eighth grade year to midway through my sophomore season. I closely observed Coach Kurzen during this time, and again was amazed by his ability to remain calm in the face of adversity and still be an outspoken follower of Jesus. I know Coach took a lot of heat during those couple of years but never once did I feel he took it out on his players. Instead, he continually encouraged us to work harder and convinced us that we had the talent to be very good.

The tide turned during my last two years of high school, going 33-10 and sharing a league championship my senior year. Coach still displayed the same calm demeanor in winning and exhibited grace to the people who had doubted him during the losing streak but had now suddenly become his biggest fans. Coach also still kept after me from a spiritual perspective, encouraging me to participate in FCA and to develop a deep relationship with Jesus Christ. I think in my head I agreed with what Coach was telling me but I don't know if I understood it in my heart. I still felt like I could handle things on my own, not knowing if I really needed a Savior.

I was about to receive a wake-up call in college.

COLLEGE LOWS

I began my college career at Case Western Reserve University with a desire to play basketball and baseball while obtaining a degree in metallurgical engineering. After one semester, things on the basketball court didn't work out, and while I made the baseball team and looked forward to playing a lot my freshman year, I did not achieve the needed grade point average to play. For what felt like the first time in my life, I was a failure. It became crystal clear that I found my worth in performance and as long as I performed well in sports or academics, I was okay. But with both sports and school seemingly taken away from me, I wasn't sure what was next.

Confused and defeated, I returned home for break and gravitated toward the one place I had always found my solace and worth: the gym. I still remember Coach Kurzen greeting me with open arms, and he really didn't care about my grade point average or how basketball was going for me. Coach cared much more about how I was doing spiritually. I had to admit that I had not felt close to God in a long time, seemingly having no place in my busy life for a relationship with Him. Coach quickly reminded me that Jesus needed to be my first priority, that He desires to be on the throne of our lives. I, on the other hand, had placed myself on the throne.

For the first time, I finally realized the truth of these words in my heart and not just my head. I, like everyone else, was a sinner who could not save himself, needing the death and resurrection of Jesus for the atonement of my sins. I accepted His free gift of salvation and felt an indescribable peace and joy as I now sought to honor Jesus in everything I did.

I finished up my undergraduate degree at Manchester College in Indiana while playing collegiate baseball and a whole lot of pick-up and intramural basketball. During these years in the mid-'80s, the Cavaliers were never much of a threat to win the championship but it was still fun to follow the exploits of the likes of World B. Free, Foots Walker and Mike Mitchell.

A CAREER AND A CALLING

After college and one semester of law school, God directed my steps to a career in child welfare. I became a case manager for a Christian foster care agency, where I developed a heart for children from hard places. Coming from a family that had always loved and supported me, it was sobering to now work with children whose families had been fractured or had never existed in the first place. My growing faith allowed me to see hope in these children. Their resiliency through difficulty inspired me, even though there were times that the desperation of the situation nearly overwhelmed me.

One of those times occurred late on a Friday night. I received an emergency referral from Portage County Department of Human Services. Two young boys, ages 5 and 6, needed placed that evening. I quickly began going through our list of foster parents and looking for anyone that would even entertain a call in the middle of the night about these boys. After making a couple of calls and becoming more and more concerned that we would not have anyone for these children, I struck pay dirt: A single foster mother from New Philadelphia agreed to take the boys. I took off from my home in Massillon, drove 45 minutes to pick the boys up in Ravenna and then made the hour-long drive to the foster mom's house in New Philadelphia.

As the boys got situated in the back of my car, I realized that they were scared, hungry and unsure about me. While driving, I began to ask them questions and share funny stories. They soon relaxed and chuckled at my or their own funny stories. By this time, it was late and I thought the boys had dozed off, when I heard a little voice from the backseat ask softly, "Mister, are you going to be our new daddy?" With tears welling up in my eyes, I replied, "No, but I am going to take you to a home where you will be safe until we can find the right place for you."

I can't tell you just how greatly that question has affected my life. Those boys still enter my mind, 20 years later, when I think about why I do what I do today, giving hope to the hopeless and helping children like them experience their worth in Christ. That drive to New Philly also cemented my belief in how important fathers are to their children's development.

LESSONS AT THE COLISEUM

For Cavaliers' fans, the early to mid-'90s were full of highlights, from the likes of Mark Price, Brad Daugherty, Larry Nance, Craig Ehlo, Hot Rod Williams, Ron Harper and Mike Sanders. These Cavs were a joy to watch, from Price's unlimited range, to Daugherty filling the lane on a fast break with a right-handed jam to Nance blocking a shot into the stands, this team had all the pieces to bring the Cavs the long-awaited championship. Unlike the Father's Day Miracle, though, it seemed like these Cavs could never catch the big break they needed to win it all.

From health issues (Rick Mahorn elbowing Price in the head) to big shots (Michael Jordan's jumper over Ehlo) to having to beat arguably the greatest player ever (Jordan), the Cavs of that era simply couldn't get it done. Yet I believe they will always be remembered as a great team made up of quality individuals. Price was my favorite, both for how he played basketball and how he represented Jesus to the world. I also still remember having the pleasure of hearing Daugherty share his testimony following a Cavs game one night. It gave me goose bumps.

Around this time, God taught me another very valuable lesson and, yes, it occurred at a Cavs game in the Coliseum. First, I need to confess that while I loved working with foster children and foster parents, I routinely struggled to connect with one type of child. I call them the "IDC" kids: "I Don't Care." These kids did not respond to any attempts at connecting with them. Whether it was praise, rewards or consequences, their simple answer was "I don't care." I admit my frustration grew when I saw massive unrealized potential in a child.

Paul was one of my IDC kids. At 17, Paul had been through a lot in his life and there was nobody waiting for him at home. He was smart and athletic, having run cross country in high school, but at some point, Paul developed the IDC attitude and gave up trying.

As a result, Paul began making bad choices and his foster family grew more and more frustrated with him. The last time I saw Paul, I was escorting him out of the foster family's home after they requested his removal, and Paul kept repeating, "I don't care about you, I don't care about anybody!" I was definitely frustrated when Paul got in the car to leave: frustrated with myself for not being able to help him and frustrated with Paul and all his arrested potential. I honestly could not say that I was sorry to see him leave.

Fast forward several years. Lori and I are sitting in the nosebleed section at the Coliseum, straining to follow the action below, when I hear my name being called. I scan the area and see a hot dog vendor climbing the steps toward me. My first thought was that I had eaten so many hot dogs, the vendors now knew me by name. As I looked closer, though, I realized it was IDC Paul! Initially, I was a little reserved in light of our last meeting, but Paul wasn't. Instead, he came up and gave me a big hug and wanted to thank me for all I had done for him. As my mouth gaped, Paul went on to tell me that he was signed up to enter the Marines the following week, and that he finally understood what his foster parents and I had been trying to tell him.

By this time, my eyes had begun to fill with tears, and I initiated the goodbye hug. As I sat back down and tried to return my attention to the game, I realized that I had just learned a valuable lesson: I am not in control; God is. God showed me that my job is to be His ambassador and allow Him to be in control of the timing. I wish I could say that, after this clear lesson, control has never again been an issue for me, but I can't. I realize that I am a control freak and need to die every day in order to turn things over to God. I also realize that many times when we say, "I don't care," we are really making a plea for help.

PROUD PARENTS

Basketball continued to be a love of mine following college as I began playing at the YMCA, on different men's teams, refereeing and coaching. I really enjoyed watching kids develop a passion for the game and its fundamentals. Once Lori and I had children – first our daughter, Hailey, and then four years later, our son, Blaine – I even started playing at 6:00 each morning with a group of about 25 other guys so I could be home with my family in the evening. The friendships that developed during those mornings endure today.

I don't think I can accurately describe the joy it has been for me to watch my children grow up. First, Blaine and Hailey are blessed to have Lori as their mom, as I am to have her as a wife. Lori is passionate about Jesus and showing His love to others. Second, they both have developed their own faith journey and it is exciting to see God utilize their gifts to build His Kingdom. Hailey began playing basketball in grade school and enjoyed playing Upward at a local church. She would eventually, however, follow in her mother's shoes by excelling at volleyball.

A record-setting high school career as a setter was followed by a couple of years at Grace College in Indiana. Hailey is a born leader on and off the volleyball court and it was a gift to watch her play, but her career was sidetracked by a serious case of mononucleosis during her sophomore year. Soon thereafter, she returned home to marry her high school sweetheart, Brandon, and began working at the church she grew up in, Abundant Life Christian Fellowship. Hailey has also done a wonderful job coaching volleyball at Tuslaw, leading the ninth grade team and helping out with the varsity setters.

Our youngest child, Blaine, grew up with a basketball in his hands. Blaine's first taste of competitive basketball was in kindergarten in Upward. Blaine was one of the youngest kids on the team but I still remember the first time he touched the ball in a game. He fired up a jumper that hit nothing but net, and he just stood there smiling.

It may have been that same year that our family had the opportunity to participate in an on-court contest at a Cavs game. As we walked into the arena, we were approached by a Cavs representative to participate in a contest during the game. The representative asked Hailey first if she would be interested and she politely declined. He then turned to Blaine. I really think Blaine was too young to understand exactly what was happening, but he agreed to participate.

So the contest went like this: There were three families chosen, each with a young child. The fathers were to dribble from the baseline to half-court and pass the ball to their wives, who had to then make a layup. After the successful layup, the child had to put on LeBron James' game jersey and shoes and run the whole length of the court. The Cavs' rep informed us that the contest would occur during a timeout in the third quarter. He asked us to report to the floor at halftime where we would have time to warm up. As a bonus, we would watch the third quarter from floor seats.

I have to admit that there were some butterflies as the game progressed through the first two quarters but by halftime, our family had our game faces on.

I'm pretty sure Lori and I were worried because we didn't want to make a mistake in front of thousands of people, but Blaine just thought it was a cool experience.

The third quarter began and soon the whistle blew. After we hustled into position, they handed me the ball on the baseline. Lori went and stood around the opposite three-point line and Blaine stood waiting at the other baseline. The buzzer sounded and I took off dribbling, passing the ball to Lori at half court. She took two dribbles and hit her first layup while the other two ladies missed theirs. At this point, we're way ahead of the pack. Lori hustled over and helped Blaine put on LeBron's jersey and large shoes, and he began clomping down the court. Blaine quickly built up a half-court lead and I was cheering him on, believing the win was in the bag.

Then Blaine made a mistake: He looked back to see where his competition was and at that moment, the girl in second place tripped in LeBron's large shoes. Blaine, his incredible compassion on full display, stopped and began turning around to help her. Of course, being the all-wise and compassionless father, I yelled at Blaine to finish the race and *then* go back to help his competitors. I don't know if I am proud or not about the fact that he did turn back around to finish, and we easily won. Blaine was still worrying about his fellow contestant after the race and he convinced me to buy her a frozen lemonade. We, on the other hand, won a flat-screen TV!

BASKETBALL BLAINE

I'm sure it wasn't easy for Hailey or Blaine growing up with me as their dad. I was never blessed with great athletic skills, but I have been blessed with a motor that won't quit. I placed high expectations on both children and wanted them to utilize all the ability God gave them to the fullest. I encouraged them to play sports as if they were playing them for Jesus, but I'm sure both Hailey and Blaine could recall times I didn't act very Christ-like, whether while reacting to a referee's calls or a coach's decisions, or commanding my son to show less compassion to a fellow competitor during a silly race. It was during those times that I had to often ask forgiveness from my children for my actions.

Even though our family supported Tuslaw, Lori and I felt God leading us to send Hailey to Kingsway Christian School where she would spend all 13 years of her education. Hailey had a fantastic experience at Kingsway and Lori and I were grateful for the relationships developed there. Blaine also began his school career at Kingsway, but in fourth grade we noticed a change. While playing basketball and baseball in the Tuslaw/Massillon area, Blaine began developing relationships with his teammates. Many of his teammates started asking him about coming to Tuslaw and Blaine found himself mulling over that possibility. It wasn't until the beginning of his seventh grade year that we finally decided to make the change, complicated by the fact it was Hailey's senior year at Kingsway. Blaine, though, had a strong desire to be a witness to his classmates at Tuslaw and wanted an opportunity to play sports for my alma mater.

Blaine entered seventh grade at Tuslaw already playing on two AAU basketball teams, and his love for the game continued to grow. In the winter season, he played for Tuslaw while preparing for the spring AAU season. With Hailey competing in JO volleyball in the winter/spring, weekends were a busy time for our family, but we loved it as we developed relationships with other families and enjoyed spending time together in hotels and sharing meals.

I should mention that Blaine's future brother-in-law, Brandon Jurkovich, also was developing a passion for basketball during this time. Brandon did not have the opportunity to start playing as early as others, but his natural athletic ability and passion for the game allowed him to quickly catch up with his peers. He also played AAU basketball, so Lori, Hailey and I often found ourselves running from one of Blaine's games to catch Brandon play.

Tuslaw hired a new varsity basketball coach Blaine's freshman year, Kevin Lower. Coach Lower selected Jim Kurzen as one of his assistant coaches, the same Coach Kurzen who was so instrumental to my growth as a basketball player and Christian. Coach and I had remained close through the years and I was so pumped for him to have the opportunity to coach my son nearly 30 years after coaching me!

Coach Kurzen also still led the FCA group at Tuslaw. Now they met at 7:00 in the morning with more than 100 kids showing up every week. Just imagine the number of kids who have been exposed to the Gospel of Christ because of Coach Kurzen's faithfulness in all of these years.

While it was exciting to watch Blaine's endeavors on the court at Tuslaw, it was even more encouraging to see his heart for his friends and classmates. When Blaine was in eighth grade, he asked Lori and me if it would be okay to have a couple of his friends over one night. We agreed, and the "couple" became 25-30 junior high kids eating, laughing and playing at our house. Blaine would take time each week to share something that God put on his heart. These gatherings continued throughout Blaine's four years in high school, and they were enhanced when Hailey began coaching volleyball and developing relationships with the girls.

My favorite "dad" moments during Blaine's high school days occurred far from the spotlight. It could be late on a weeknight during the summer, or a lazy Sunday afternoon in the fall, and Blaine would ask if we could go shoot at the gym. First, we had to see if we could get the keys from someone, usually Coach Kurzen or Hailey, and then we had to make sure no one else was using the gym, and then we had to make sure the baskets were down. Then before beginning to shoot, Blaine had to ensure we had music playing, so he would cue up anything from LeCrae to Casting Crowns to Hillsong to Propaganda to Chris Tomlin, and we would begin shooting.

My main role during those times was to be the rebounder and to pass the ball back out as Blaine cut to shoot a jumper. I would often catch myself smiling, my heart full of contentment and gratitude for having this opportunity to be with Blaine, for Blaine being able to combine his love of basketball with his love of worship music, and for the privilege of watching Blaine develop into a man after God's own heart. We had time to talk about his faith, his life, girls and even basketball. Of course, then he would challenge me to play one on one at the end of our shooting sessions. This was more enjoyable during his junior high years when I could still hold my own, but by the time he reached high school, it became more and more difficult to keep up with him!

SUCCESS AT TUSLAW

It seems Blaine's high school years were over in the blink of an eye. He and his teammates had the normal ups and downs throughout their four years, including tension early on about whether the underclassmen should get more playing time or if upperclassmen deserved more minutes because they had seniority. While Lori and I often struggled with coaching decisions during those years, I don't recall Blaine ever responding with a negative comment about his coaches or teammates. He was more focused on the results on the court.

After winning a district championship in Blaine's junior year, Tuslaw, entered the 2015-16 basketball campaign with extremely high expectations, much like the Cavaliers. Their non-league schedule had been strengthened with Division I opponents that would challenge the team and Tuslaw met every test before ultimately finishing the regular season 22-0. Tuslaw was the state's #2 ranked division III team heading into the tournament, earning a #1 seed in the Salem district. Unfortunately, they lost the district final game to St. Thomas Aquinas to end their season at 25-1.

Blaine was extremely grateful for the opportunity to play for arguably the greatest team ever at Tuslaw. There were many highlights that year, but my favorite occurred during a game at Tuslaw's archrival, Fairless, when Blaine set the school record for three-pointers in a game, making 8 out of 11 shots from long range while sitting out the fourth quarter. Of course, Lori and I were proud parents that evening, but a couple of things following the game made us even prouder.

First, while walking through the handshake line, the Fairless coach pulled Blaine aside and congratulated him on his play, complimented him on his humble attitude and encouraged him to keep playing that way. Then that Sunday at church, Coach Kurzen relayed that following the game, a Fairless fan – one whom Coach had played against in high school – approached Coach, congratulated him on the win and mentioned what a joy it must be to coach Blaine each day. As much as he was impressed with his basketball ability, this Fairless fan was even more impressed with Blaine's attitude. That was one of my proudest moments as Blaine's parent and it had little to do with his basketball ability.

As I shared this story with Blaine, I mentioned that long after people forget your won-loss record or your shooting ability, they will remember your character. Lori and I have made many mistakes in raising Blaine and Hailey, but we are so grateful that we follow a God who can redeem all things, and whose grace is simply amazing.

SOMETHING TO CELEBRATE

With the Tuslaw season over, we turned our attention to the Cavs, wondering if they would be able to capture that elusive championship for their die-hard Cleveland fans. During the playoff season, the gang from Blaine's class could often be found watching the games in our basement, and you could tell the excitement was building as we made it through the Eastern Conference playoffs and once again qualified for the NBA Finals against the Warriors.

And as Game 7 wrapped up and Lori and I danced in the living room, we couldn't help but wonder how are kids were responding to the news that we were finally champions. That's right, they weren't celebrating with us in our living room; instead, Hailey, Brandon and Blaine were trying to follow the exploits of the Cavs from a cafeteria in Chilca, Peru, where their weeklong mission trip at the children's home with Esperanza de Ana had just begun.

Would I have enjoyed celebrating with my children in our home on Father's Day when the Cavs won? Sure. Was I even more grateful to Facetime with them a little later that evening when they learned the Cavs had won? You bet. While basketball may be the greatest game ever invented, our children spending time living out their faith and investing in others because of Jesus stands as an even greater legacy.

––––

ABOUT KEVIN HEWITT
Kevin is blessed to be the husband of Lori and father of Blaine, Hailey and Brandon (son-in-law), to lead the family of ministries at Christian Children's Home of Ohio, and most importantly, to continue learning how to bask in the grace of Jesus while accurately reflecting His grace to the world. In his spare time, Kevin enjoys trying to hit a little white ball where he is aiming, reading anything that inspires, and passionately following the Cleveland and OSU sports teams.

7 IN VICTORY & DEFEAT

By Ryan Heckert

CEO, The Workshops Inc.

"As a father shows compassion to his children,

so the Lord shows compassion to those who fear him."

Psalm 103:13 ESV

Despite growing up in Oklahoma, Florida and North Carolina, Cleveland sports have always been part of my life. Thanks to my father, who was born and raised in Crawford County, Ohio, I have a sense of love and loyalty to the Indians, Browns and Cavs. During good and bad times, he cheered on our teams. He celebrated the wins and always seemed to know what caused the losses.

No matter which way the wind blew, my father was always anchored to the teams that played in the City by the Lake. Not once did he ever look to abandon ship; not once did he stop cheering and hoping and believing. As a father myself now, looking back through the past 38 years, I can't help but think a little beyond just those wins and losses, a little beyond life's simple things.

I know I'm not alone when I say that God has led me through several "character building" years, and I can't help but compare my journey to some of those Cleveland teams. While I had good seasons here and there, I also had more than my fair share of losing seasons. In fact, I had quite a few!

While I see myself in those teams, I see my father in them even more, just as steady with my brother and me as he has been with those beloved teams. No matter what, he remained anchored to us. He celebrated the wins with us and helped us figure out what caused the losses. He was there for us and supported us unconditionally. No matter what we did, or how often we ran the same failed play over and over again, his steadfastness as our fan never wavered. Not one single time.

Our father's investment in us has allowed me to understand how critical and significant it is to stand strong with and for my three children. Layna, Luke and Ava are cherished gifts who create joy, happiness and, at times, a little stress, just as my brother and I did for our parents. We recently finalized our adoption of Ava, a process that has given my wife and me an even deeper appreciation for the privilege of parenthood. Our three children have had many victories and a few defeats so far in their short lives and there are so many more to come. I am determined to celebrate and support them through it all, as my father did with me.

On Father's Day in 2016, I found myself stranded in Cincinnati on the eve of a three-day work conference. Had it not been for this prior commitment, my father, brother and I would have been hunkered down in the man cave while we watched our Cavaliers pursue history in Game 7 of the NBA Finals. We would have cheered and celebrated, hugged and probably cried (but just a little).

Despite the distance between us, we did connect over a Facetime call and celebrated the miraculous championship briefly, a memory I won't soon forget. But what I'll remember more is what a remarkable earthly example of our Heavenly Father's enormous love that my dad has set and continues to display in his life. No matter our mistakes or losses – NO MATTER WHAT – my father has always been in my corner. And so has God.

ABOUT RYAN HECKERT
Ryan is a Jesus follower, a wife lover and a kid wrangler. During the day (and some nights and weekends), he gets to lead an organization that serves and supports adults with disabilities. When not engaged in the aforementioned, he golfs, plays basketball, takes pictures and thinks about survival skills.

8 BACKYARD BALL

By Joe Franz
Director of Advancement, Christian Children's Home of Ohio

"And these words that I command you today shall be on your heart.
You shall teach them diligently to your children, and shall talk of them
when you sit in your house, and when you walk by the way,
and when you lie down, and when you rise."
Deuteronomy 6:6-7 ESV

Long before Dad and I would play catch or shoot hoops in our backyard, his dad, Earl Franz Sr., did the same. Grandpa Franz lived to be 98. Born a couple of decades after the Civil War ended and before cars were popular in the U.S. – and living well beyond man landing on the moon – Grandpa saw a lot of progress.

Dad grew up on 18th Street in Canton. One day, he came home from school to see a basketball hoop mounted on the side of a small barn behind the house. Dad played competitive basketball through his freshman year in high school and the neighborhood kids would often stop over for a quick game, but some of his fondest memories were when Grandpa would take time to play – often basketball but other times tossing the football or baseball or even horseshoes. I imagine they enjoyed their time together, caught up a bit on things and dreamt some about the future.

CEMENTING OUR RELATIONSHIP

Beep...Beep...Beep. I awoke to the sounds of a large truck backing up on what used to be our blacktop driveway. I leapt from my bed to look out the window. A cement truck was getting ready to pour our new driveway, a small pad out back where a shed would be built and, to my surprise, a much larger cement area that would soon be where Dad installed our own basketball hoop. This was a big deal for our middle-income family, representing an intentional investment by Dad, influenced by his dad, to build memories and a better jump shot.

I was eight years old when Dad installed the hoop. Just like a generation before, I would spend countless hours out back with friends, pretending to be Mark Price beating the buzzer with a shot that won the NBA championship for the Cavs – still only a dream at that point. Sometimes it was just Dad and me playing a few games of Around the World or Horse after finishing the yardwork. Dad had a good shot and was tough to beat. As I think back, I can still smell the scent of our freshly cut lawn as the sky struggled to stay lit while the sun set on the other side of the house. Mom was calling the boys in for the night – we had church in the morning.

We rarely missed a Sunday at church. Dad was always up first those mornings, reading the paper before the rest of us even had breakfast. On the way out the door, he would grab his leather-bound Bible with the gold-trimmed pages and we'd all load into the car for the drive to church.

I grew up attending First Christian Church in Canton (FCC), starting in the nursery all the way through my high school years before going off to college. Some of my favorite memories include playing in the FCC Youth Basketball League. Dad came to as many games as he could, cheering us on next to Mom. Some great men, like Tony Garcia, poured into us boys, teaching us the fundamentals of basketball, how to play as a team and to always remember we were Christ's ambassadors – on and off the basketball court. Many kids would learn about Jesus for the first time while playing in our league thanks to guys like Tony and other men who cared – not just about basketball, but about passing their faith on to the next generation as well.

My father had a steady but quiet faith. He and Mom volunteered one year in the youth ministry while I was growing up, but most of Dad's volunteer efforts were connected to his Sunday school class. Dad wasn't the one saying the prayer at mealtime – that was Mom. She was really the spiritual leader of the family and I owe a lot of who I am in Christ today to her. Dad was always there too, in full agreement that passing on their Christian faith was a priority and something we valued as a family. When I accepted the Lord as my personal Savior at age 11 and was baptized at FCC, Dad was there. Years later, I would have the privilege of baptizing my fiancée, Cindy (now my wife of 23 years), and then also leading our four children to Christ, baptizing them when each was old enough to make that decision on their own. Dad was there for those as well.

AN ALL-STAR DAD

Dad would sometimes score tickets to sporting events. My fondest memories are walking the beautiful Firestone Country Club while watching the best golfers in the world play in the World Series of Golf or heading up to the Coliseum to watch a Cavs game. I got to see Jack Nicklaus play – one of the last times he'd compete at Firestone – and actually got his autograph on my GlenOak High School golf team visor. In the mid-'80s, World B. Free was raining jump shots from all over the court. It seemed like his shots were in the air forever and then – *swish* – through the hoop they'd go. The Cavs weren't that good but it sure was fun going up to the games once in a while.

Later, we'd cheer on Mark Price, Brad Daugherty, Larry Nance, Craig Ehlo, Hot Rod Williams and, for a while, Ron Harper. This was our best chance yet to win it all, and there were many reasons to be excited and believe. I can still remember my favorite Cavs t-shirt with drawings of all those guys on it – I wore it everywhere! Ultimately, we fell just short to the great Chicago Bulls teams of the era, when guys like Michael Jordan and Scottie Pippen were becoming legends.

I had more success with golf than I did basketball. After a successful YBA run at the YMCA and some church basketball, I got cut from my seventh grade team. My basketball career was over. My older brothers, Brad and Tim, lived in Texas at the time but kept in touch with me. I remember them actually coordinating with Mom and Dad and paying for my golf membership at Edgewood Golf Course for a couple of years so I could practice. It paid off: After missing the team by one stroke my freshman year, I made the team my sophomore year and had a successful varsity run during my junior and senior years. Dad and I hit the links together once in a while and, on occasion, I would fill in as a sub for someone during his work golf league. I think Dad was kind of proud of my game.

Eventually, high school ended and, with it, my competitive golf career. The University of Akron came next, where I would meet Cindy and earn a business degree. When a new job took me to Wisconsin after graduation, my brother Tim sent me a leather-bound Bible with gold-trimmed pages. Just like Dad's. For years, Dad had shown us the value of keeping our priorities straight and Tim wanted to make sure those lessons would not be forgotten now that I was away from home. I still have that Bible. After telling Tim that my roommate, Doug Walter, needed a Bible, he sent one to Doug too. If more is caught than taught, I guess you could say Dad figured out how to throw us the ball.

NOW IT'S MY TURN

Early on in our marriage – even before we got married – Cindy and I decided we would raise our children in the Christian faith. As our children were born – first Susan, then Lauren, followed by Andrew and Joshua – we would often discuss our family values. We decided that faith, family and fitness were high on our list and that we would intentionally invest in these values as parents. Just like Dad had instilled in me through modeling faith, prioritizing family and encouraging fitness through sports, I would do the same.

It hasn't been easy, but our marriage is stronger today than it's ever been. We've had our highs and our lows but through it all, our faith has sustained us. I've realized that being a good husband is intricately connected to being a successful father. As men, one of the best things we can do for our children is to cherish their mother and model Christ's love to our wives. Just as important to remember: While we have much to learn from our earthly fathers – the good and the not so good – we can always turn to our Heavenly Father for guidance, wisdom, and the true love that our wives and kids so deeply yearn for from us.

You're never really "ready" to be a dad; you just kind of jump in and give it your best shot. I'm thankful for the example I have in my dad. He loves my two brothers and me a lot, and continues to provide and care for Mom (Jo Ann) as he has for more than 50 years now. As a dad myself, I quickly talk about each of my kids when asked about my family. I'll often start with their grade in school and what they're up to – typically in athletics.

Susan is our swimmer, just finishing her third year on the swim team at the University of Akron. Lauren graduates from GlenOak this year, having been a varsity cheerleader and gymnast while most recently taking up diving. When all is said and done, it's my prayer that my girls will continue to grow in their faith and marry men that will model Christ's love to them and their kids.

As for my boys, I pray they will grow up to be men of faith, instilling the same values in their families and continuing to pass on their love for Jesus to the next generation. Andrew, a sophomore, plays basketball and golf. My youngest, Josh, is finishing sixth grade and plays soccer. This basketball season was particularly special because, on Senior Night, we walked with Lauren before watching Andrew start his JV game. It was a night to remember.

Each of our kids has had some defining moments in their athletic quests but perhaps none tested their character as much as when Andrew was cut from the freshman basketball team. He has played competitive basketball ever since opening up the Little Tikes hoop one Christmas morning, and he and I have hoisted up countless shots on that old cement pad behind my childhood home, Dad often watching from a nearby chair. Through Yball, Little Eagles (elementary) and travel teams, Andrew has been on a lot of winning teams. He's attended basketball camps and found success through several seasons of AAU ball, playing meaningful minutes throughout middle school. Then one day it was over.

I'll never forget how he handled it. Sure, he was depressed. Who wouldn't be? But he took it in stride. He didn't dwell on it. We talked about it a little, but not a lot. Then one day, he started going back to the gym. He was working out day and night, playing in some pick-up games at the Edgewood Community Center or practicing on our portable hoop at home. After a coaching change at the high school, Andrew tried out again this year and earned a spot on the team. His hard work had paid off. I'm not sure if his handles will carry him as far as his player in "NBA2K17" on the Xbox, but that's not important. The life lessons he learned from this experience will undoubtedly impact him – and possibly generations of kids after him, if he gets his chance to coach someday.

Everyone in our family likes basketball and we're all Cavaliers fans. We've been to quite a few games over the years, including some of LeBron James' early years with the Cavs and a few upon his return. We've experienced the highs and the lows of supporting our team. A couple of times, we even got to see Lauren and her cheer squad perform at the Q before a Cavs game. Needless to say, we were all holding our collective breath as LeBron led his teammates through the 2016 Eastern Conference playoffs before fighting back from a 3-games-to-1 deficit in the NBA Finals to force a Game 7 on Father's Day. The stage was set.

CELEBRATING FATHER'S DAY

Dad was 36 years old the last time a Cleveland sports team won a championship – the 1964 Browns. He wasn't married yet and I was still five years away from entering this world, so a lot has changed for our family in the 52 years since. *Everything* changed for Cleveland fans on Father's Day 2016.

We started the day at church and then gathered together, like we always have, to celebrate Father's Day. We gave thanks to the Lord and enjoyed a good meal before giving gifts to the dads in the family. So, what do you get a dad who's in his 80s and has been blessed in so many ways already? How about an unprecedented Game 7 win inside Oracle Arena in Oakland, California against the defending champions, the Golden State Warriors, who just lit up the NBA with the best regular season in history? THAT would be my dad's gift on this Father's Day, and mine too!

The funny thing is, although we'd watched many games together, we weren't together for this one. After our traditional gathering earlier that day, we all headed in different directions. Cindy went to work and my kids went back home or back to college. Andrew was away at Summer in the Son, a weeklong experience for high school students to grow in their Christian faith, and streamed the game live on his phone, even though he wasn't supposed to. And yes, it was right in the middle of one of the weekend worship services. Imagine standing up to praise Jesus, singing a worship song, while at the same time watching the final minutes of Game 7!

As the room grew quiet and it became clear that the Cavs had secured the victory, Andrew shouted, "They won! The Cavs won!" Sure, technically Andrew was breaking the rules...but we let this one slide. I'm pretty sure the angels in heaven were watching too. The Man Upstairs was smiling on Cleveland that day. I exchanged a few texts before Andrew got his phone taken away for the rest of the retreat. We'll never forget it.

I was watching the game with my two brothers, a special moment in time. When LeBron completed his chase-down block and Kyrie sank that late 3-pointer, it was as if time stood still. I kept thinking, this isn't really happening. But it was happening, and we high-fived and jumped around the room like we were little kids. It was late, but we watched every minute of the post-game coverage. We just wanted to soak up the moment.

I called Dad the next day and we talked about the game, reliving every detail of the closing minutes and how it felt to see them win. We knew this was huge for so many reasons. It would almost immediately impact Cleveland and the greater northeast Ohio area in a positive way. The so-called curse had been broken.

A few months later, I went to Mom and Dad's hoping to watch the Indians complete an encore performance in Game 7 of the World Series. That night, I was struck by how different things seemed for the city and us fans. The Cavs winning in June gave everyone hope that the Indians could pull it off too. And though they lost their own Game 7 to the Chicago Cubs that night, something fascinating happened afterward: Our newfound hope never wavered. The Cavs proved that anything is possible, and one disappointing setback could not and would not diminish that truth.

In a similar way, Dad showed my brothers and me that, with God, anything is possible. I look at my marriage, my kids, the way Andrew so admirably handled the biggest disappointment of his young life, and I see Dad's example of consistency, perseverance and steady leadership shining through. I pray that I continue to build on that example for Cindy and my kids, and that Susan, Lauren, Andrew and Joshua do the same when it's their turn. The next generation depends on it.

———

ABOUT JOE FRANZ
My life purpose is to glorify God by bringing His ideas to fruition. I've held leadership roles in the business community, my local church and now at Christian Children's Home of Ohio – a nonprofit. I'm passionate about: my faith, my family and making

an impact in our community. Oh, and sports, good coffee and all things marketing/communications. I like to hit the links once in a while and enjoy a good book. If you look, you'll find me on social media too.

9 OVERCOMING THE DISTANCE

By Will Van Nostran
President of Operations, Van Nostran Young & Associates

"Train up a child in the way he should go;
even when he is old he will not depart from it."
Proverbs 22:6 NIV

The story of my relationship with my father is one of redemption. The same could be said about the story of Cleveland's pro sports teams.

It was painfully cold that January day, with reported temperatures at old Municipal Stadium reaching as low as 4°F. But we didn't care – about the temperature or the visiting Oakland Raiders. We had Brian Sipe, Reggie Rucker, Greg Pruitt, Ozzie Newsome and the rest of the Kardiac Kids.

The Browns had won their first division title in nine years that season, going 11-5 and authoring some incredible late-game heroics that earned them their iconic nickname. On this day in 1981, Municipal Stadium was sold out (as it always was) for the Browns' AFC divisional playoff game against the Raiders. I was 11 and I was excited, as much about the game as I was about whom I was with: Dad.

My parents had divorced five years earlier. Divorce wasn't as prevalent then as it is today, so there were times when I was singled out for having only one parent. My mother helped me navigate those difficult moments, in large part by making sure I was in church every week and providing the kind of steady guidance and love I desperately needed at that time. On the other hand, I didn't see Dad very often those days, and as a result, our relationship was distant. When we were together, though, our time typically involved two things: faith and sports.

Dad has never been the biggest Browns fan, but he definitely rooted for them and did his best to take me to games when the opportunities were available. More significantly, though, Dad was very purposeful about instilling in me the importance of faith and investing in my relationship with God. As I got older and our own relationship matured, he would share with me the ways his faith had pulled him through a very difficult time during the divorce.

I may not have been close with my dad growing up but his impact on my life continues to reverberate to this day. My wife, Sue, and I both come from divorced families so we promised each other that we wouldn't make the same mistakes in our marriage that our parents did. Because we have been committed to fostering meaningful connections within our family, I enjoy the sort of bond with my two children, Drake and Lily, that I never had as a kid with my father. The distance between my father and me growing up has given me clear purpose and direction in my own journey as a father, and I'm able to talk about things with my kids that I never had the opportunity to share with my dad.

But Dad's persistence in discussing his faith and helping me better understand mine has helped me to be an open book with Drake and Lily. He allowed me to see the ways his faith sustained him and enhanced his life, and now I not only get to pass that down to my kids but I often find myself amazed by Drake's faith. It's so powerful to see a young man walk with God, and his actions as he navigates through his own life have helped me learn to be better for my family.

We follow the Great Redeemer, and for that I am so thankful. The divorce could have shattered my relationship with both parents but instead, I have so many great memories from those days with Mom, who was my rock for so long. Dad and I, meanwhile, enjoy a very good relationship today, and his relationship with Drake is special. The three of us love to golf together and I often see him being the kind of role model for Drake that he never was really able to be for me.

And yet, despite our flawed and sometimes painful past, Dad taught me that my sacrifices in life should be for my family and not to fulfill my own self interests, an invaluable lesson that inspires Sue and me to work hard so our kids have the opportunities and experience the kinds of relationships that we did not.

I will always be grateful to my dad for how he intentionally stayed connected with me despite the divorce, and even though the Browns lost on that frigid January day in 1981, I also am grateful that he took me to that historic game. Who knew at the time that "Red Right 88," as it quickly became known as, would soon be followed by so many painful losses by the Browns ("The Drive" and "The Fumble"), the Cavaliers ("The Shot" and "The Decision") and the Indians (the 1997 World Series)? Fortunately, 35 years after the Kardiac Kids fell to the Raiders, LeBron James and the Cavaliers brought Cleveland fans their long-awaited shot at redemption, a joyful moment I shared with Sue, Drake and Lily on Father's Day.

Sue cooked up some great food for the game and the four of us glued ourselves to the TV, ready to witness history. The game progressed; the excitement built. One question crept into my mind: "Is this really going to happen?" Everyone talks about LeBron's block and Kyrie Irving's winning three, but after Kevin Love played shutdown defense on Steph Curry to preserve the Cavs' late lead, I said to Drake, "Extraordinary people do extraordinary things when they put their mind to it." I've always appreciated the vital teaching moments sports can provide, and this game reinforced the value of dreaming big, working hard and having a purpose in all things.

The final seconds ticked off the clock but in our house, the celebration was delayed a few moments while we all sat there, shocked, making sure it was all real. It was, of course, and we soon found ourselves celebrating a moment that northeast Ohio families had been dreaming about for 52 years.

Decades of suffering, finally redeemed.

ABOUT WILL VAN NOSTRAN

Born and raised in Canton, 1989 graduate of GlenOak HS and Kent State graduate. Husband to Sue Van Nostran and father to Lily and Drake. Enjoys outside activities and spending time with friends and family.

10 DRU, BRON & A SACRED RESPONSIBILITY

By Dru Joyce II
Head Boys Basketball Coach, St. Vincent- St. Mary High School

"For you know how, like a father with his children, we exhorted each one of you and encouraged you and charged you to walk in a manner worthy of God, who calls you into his own kingdom and glory."
1 Thessalonians 2:11-12 ESV

I saw him coming.

There are just under two minutes to go in Game 7 of the 2016 NBA Finals. Andre Iguodala and Steph Curry are racing down the floor on a fast break that threatens to unknot the 87-87 tie. J.R. Smith stands on a lonely island in front of the streaking Warriors teammates. A short pass from Iguodala to Curry followed by a quick bounce pass back to Iguodala has Smith all turned around. The bucket looks inevitable, unless you happen to notice #23 streaking in from behind the play on a mission to make history.

I saw LeBron James coming that night because I saw him make incredible plays like that chase-down block dozens of times when I coached him, my son Dru Joyce III and their teammates at St. Vincent-St. Mary High School in Akron,

Ohio. Sure, many of those plays over the years happened during games, but I wish I had recorded some of our practices from those early days because they could get incredibly intense.

I used to shake things up by teaming Bron with the second-stringers and having them scrimmage against the starters. They were all so competitive back then – you have to be to win a state championship – but these scrimmages really brought out the fire in them.

Anyone who knows anything about LeBron James the pro shouldn't be surprised to know that his will to win was just as strong when I coached him in high school, but my oldest son, Dru, may be the only person I know who is even more competitive than Bron. So when these two best of friends faced off in my scrimmages, it wasn't uncommon for actual fights to break out, with each side doing everything they could to win. And more often than not, Bron would make some kind of memorable play for his team with the game on the line. A play just like "The Block" on Iguodala that helped the Cavaliers complete their improbable comeback on their way to the franchise's first championship.

Watching Bron celebrate on the floor with his teammates that night gave me a special kind of joy, knowing how important this championship was to him, how badly he wanted to bring a title to the people in northeast Ohio. You could see the pressure being lifted as the tears streamed unapologetically down his face that night. Dru told Bron a couple days before Game 7 that he wouldn't be able to control his emotions if the Cavaliers came out on top. Boy, was he right!

As you might guess, I consider myself incredibly fortunate to have had the opportunity to coach Bron, Dru and their teammates back then, but to me, coaching is about so much more than X's and O's or wins and losses. As my career developed, I started to understand that the Lord had entrusted me with a sacred responsibility, that I have the privilege of pouring my life into kids at a very impactful age, many of whom need a mentor even more than they need a coach. It's a responsibility that largely defines who I am as a coach and influences the man I have become in many other areas of my life. Of course, it took quite a long time before I was ready to accept this kind of responsibility.

MOM, DAD AND EAST LIVERPOOL

Long before that state championship with Bron and Dru, before my own children were born, before my wife and I were ever married, and before I came to know the Lord myself, there was a tiny wooden house on a steep dirt hill in East Liverpool, Ohio.

I never knew how little we had growing up in that small town along the Ohio River. Our house at the top of the hill was heated by a coal furnace, and a good storm would send us scurrying for buckets to catch the water leaking through the old roof. We didn't even own a car until I was in eighth grade, instead walking or riding the bus wherever we went. But my parents worked for what we did have.

They married late in life and had me soon after that – my mother at 40 and my father at 38. Mom worked very hard as a housekeeper so I could have different things, and looking back, I can see that I inherited my work ethic from her. My dad, meanwhile, was the kind of guy that everyone liked. He spent years working as a janitor in a bank and jewelry store, but unfortunately, my mother expected more from him. East Liverpool isn't far from Pittsburgh, and a lot of people in town worked for the steel mill in Midland, Pennsylvania. Not Dad. He enjoyed his life and didn't want to give up his long lunches at the pool hall.

Because of that, he and my mother had a tumultuous kind of relationship, and her resentment splashed onto me. She would say things like, "Your dad ain't doing nothing. He gave up on life. Don't be like him." Even worse, he just kind of took it, which made it easy for me to simply side with my mother. I started believing the things she said and developing my own negative feelings about him. I never voiced them to him, but I wasn't real proud of him as a dad.

Their relationship deteriorated even more when I went off to college. He started drifting farther away from the house and spending more and more time at the bar because, frankly, home wasn't a nice place to be. And when he was there, he would be in one chair dozing off and my mother would be in the other chair, one eye on the TV and one on him.

RESCUED IN A TRAILER

I would love to say that I inherited my passion for sports from my father, but aside from the Sunday afternoons we spent watching the Browns play, he wasn't much of a sports fan. Instead, I became a football fan the old fashioned way: I played it.

Growing up in East Liverpool, there wasn't a whole lot to keep boys occupied. My cousins and I latched on to football and I never let go, playing through high school with every intention of continuing in college. My initial plan was to play at Ashland University but I didn't stay there long, transferring to Ohio University in search of more: more people, more parties, more fun.

I found what I was looking for on OU's Athens campus but it ended up being much more than I'd bargained for. Girls and parties became my focus; my grades and my relationships suffered. I was chasing everything my peers told me was important, and yet I was lost. Entering my senior year, my life was quickly unraveling.

I had been a somewhat typical church kid growing up. We attended a traditional African Methodist Episcopal (AME) church in East Liverpool, where I learned how to look like a good person who could tell you all about the stories in the Bible.

My mother led Sunday school for many years, and later I spent some time teaching Sunday school classes because that's what good church kids did. I was outwardly righteous and I knew how to play the part, as many high school kids do, but I wasn't saved. I didn't think I needed to be saved.

In September of my senior year at Ohio University, it became clear how wrong I was. I found myself staring into a mirror in the small trailer I was living in and not liking who I saw staring back at me. In my quest to satisfy my own desires and prove to anyone who would bother to notice that I was just as cool as everyone else on campus, I had selfishly tried to carry on a relationship with multiple women at once, which ended up causing all of them unnecessary pain. My decisions created my environment, and in front of that fogged up mirror in that tiny trailer, my environment looked pretty bleak and, ironically, rather lonely.

Before I fully understood what was happening, I began praying: "Lord, please come into my life and help me be the person You want me to be." On that day, in that trailer, God made it clear that my time of acting without regard for consequences or the feelings of others was over. At that moment, my life forever changed. God began working in me in powerful and profound ways, first by showing me how broken and lost I had become without Him.

Soon thereafter, I began to make things right with one of the women I had hurt previously, and after months of proving to her that I had truly changed and was committed to following the Lord in all things, Carolyn agreed to marry me. Just as my decisions had created a destructive environment previously, God used my salvation decision in that trailer to create a brand new, redeemed environment that, nearly 40 years later, I continue to share with my soul mate.

ETERNITY FOR DAD

While I can trace the origin of my faith back to those times spent in the AME church, Sundays were my mother's thing; my father didn't attend church with us. I've often wondered how his life may have been different if he had.

Not very long after Carolyn and I got married, my father had a stroke, a scary moment that eventually led to one of my most cherished memories. After he recovered from the stroke, he and I sat in our old East Liverpool home and he admitted being scared, wondering what was next in life for him. "I'm just going to go back and do what I've been doing," he said. I told him there was a better way. "If you believe that Jesus is God's Son and that He died for our sins," I said, "let's make this confession right here." And he did.

A couple years later, Dad suffered another stroke. Sitting with him in the hospital, I started examining some of the feelings about him that I'd been carrying for nearly my whole life. This second stroke woke me up and reminded me that life isn't promised. You just never know how long you have.

So I started reflecting on who my father actually was. What did he really mean to me? Was he really that bad of a father? Truthfully, he was always there for me. Every football game, every track meet, whatever I did, he was always there. No, he didn't make a lot of money but if I needed a dollar or two, he gave me what he had. My opinion of him, I now saw, was unfair.

As a coach, I've been around so many kids who don't have a dad in their lives, or who have a dad who isn't involved, who isn't present and active with them. That wasn't my dad. He was always present. By the time I got to high school, we had a little car. It wasn't the greatest thing but whenever I had an away football game, he was driving that little car to the field, no matter how far away it was. He was there.

I had to come to terms with that. I needed to be careful about how I viewed things. I had taken on my mother's perspective about who my dad was, and in those moments I realized there was so much more to being a dad than what she wanted as a husband. As a husband, he may not have measured up to what my mom wanted, but as a dad? He absolutely measured up to what I needed, and he taught me how important it is to not only be there for my four kids, but to be involved in their lives.

Looking back on that time, my father's two strokes forever changed our lives and our relationship, because after leading him to faith following his first stroke, I found myself apologizing to him in the hospital, on his deathbed, after his second stroke for the way I had felt about him for so long. I told him that I loved him and that I was sorry for being so unfair to him. We were able to bridge the gap that had opened between us, which meant so much to him but even more to me because I was the one who harbored the negativity. He passed not long after that, and I'm so grateful not only for being able to share that powerful moment of healing and reconciliation with him, but also for being a part of his eternal decision to turn his life over to the Lord.

PRESENT AND ACCOUNTABLE

The things I learned through that time and in my moments of reflection have dramatically shaped who I am as a father. After recognizing all the ways Dad supported me, I just wanted to be there for my kids when I became a dad, whatever they did. I'd drive my daughters to dance and gymnastics and marvel at what they were able to do. I had the opportunity to coach Dru and my youngest son Cameron into high school, and through that time we created the Northeast Ohio Basketball Association. I've made it my business to be involved in all their lives, and I have my father to thank for that.

Of course, it hasn't always been easy, particularly for Dru and me. He played tennis and football early on, along with basketball. I tried to turn him into a wide receiver but it soon became clear that he didn't have the size to keep playing football. He was a heck of a tennis player, though, like his sister India, but when his coach told an 11-year-old Dru that he had to choose between tennis and basketball, we officially became a basketball family.

Dru and I butted heads a lot during those years. I mean, we had some real knock-down-drag-outs because he's so strong-willed and he wanted to do everything his way. "No," I'd tell him, "you're going to do it my way," and I would critique him endlessly. My intentions were pure – I wanted him to be the best he could be – but Dru didn't respond well to my methods and our relationship suffered.

After coaching Dru along with Bron and their group since they were 10, the boys moved on to high school at St. Vincent-St. Mary. I joined the coaching staff as an assistant but because of the problems Dru and I had, I was relieved to see him thrive under Coach Keith Dambrot.

When Coach Dambrot moved on to the University of Akron, I took his spot and my relationship with Dru grew tumultuous again. Finally, I just asked him, "Am I being too hard on you?" He looked at me and simply said, "Yeah, you are." And I finally got it: I had been putting too much pressure on him.

Dru wasn't able to make mistakes with me. Everyone else on the team could screw up, but not Dru. After our conversation, I backed off and allowed him to make the kinds of mistakes he needed to experience so he could really start to grow as a player and a young man. Bron was without a doubt the best player on the team but Dru was our leader.

Coaching Dru and working through our problems helped me recognize that him being my son was so much sweeter than him being my player. For years, I had these blinders on that only allowed me to see Dru as a basketball player, and it stifled our relationship. The Lord helped me remove those blinders and see my son for who he really was. Later, when he went to college, Dru's first call after his games would be to me, and my first call after my games would be to him. We had come full circle.

This served as a pivotal learning experience for me as both a father and a coach. I now understood that sometimes, I needed to parent my own kids as individuals and coach my players according to their needs. One year, my coaches were telling me I should cut one particular player, a young man who had escaped ethnic cleansing in Yugoslavia with his Muslim family. This kid was brilliant – he spoke four or five different languages – but he also was a hothead who racked up countless technical fouls and generally upset our team chemistry. I didn't know what to do with him.

Driving to practice one day, the Lord just laid it on my heart: "You've got to coach him differently. You don't know what this means to him. You don't understand." The Lord was right, as He always is: I didn't understand. "He needs basketball." So I stuck with him.

We wound up winning the state championship that year, and after the season, this young man told me about problems he and his father were having, about sometimes needing to sleep in his car because he and his dad would have fistfights at night. I had no idea about any of it. He told me just how much basketball meant to him, and yet at one point I had considered cutting him. Today, he and his father have made amends and his story serves as a vivid reminder that we are accountable for the decisions we make as coaches. We have a responsibility to recognize the individual needs of the kids who come through our programs so we can best help prepare them for whatever comes next in their lives.

This has been particularly true in my experiences with boys coming from single-parent families, kids who may lack a positive male influence in their lives. Typically, these boys have a hard time with respect and authority, which you can imagine presents unique challenges for a coach. One of my former players who struggled accepting me as a male authority figure once said, "Coach Dru, I don't do well with you hollering at me." I told him that I couldn't promise I'd never raise my voice, but I also let him know that I heard him and understood. From that point forward, I would pull him aside and tell him candidly what he was doing wrong, and he flourished.

Many of these boys might be hearing a female voice of authority at home but at some point, most boys rebel against their mothers, thinking, "I'm a man, what can you do to me?" They yearn for that strong male influence to show them what it means to be a man in this world. My role is to help them grow into men.

One way I model this is through my relationship with my wife. I call Carolyn my Queen. My players have heard that for years. I want them to understand that she holds a special place, and when I need to make a decision between them and her, I'm always choosing her. "Sorry, fellas, but I'm not leaving the gym open another hour tonight. I'm going home to my Queen." They need to understand that our culture's derogatory views of women aren't right, that there's a better way. And if you do it the right way, your relationship with a woman is so much more fulfilling.

CAUGHT, NOT TAUGHT

Unfortunately, words often fall on deaf ears. Actions, on the other hand, tend to resonate and endure long after the talking ends. Through my time as a father and a coach and my interactions with young men from all different life situations, one thing has been made clear: Faith and values are caught, not taught.

We saw this early on with our children. We went to church and prayed and exposed them to all the things they needed to be exposed to, as most Christian parents do, but it wasn't personal or life changing until our kids really owned their faith. And for that to happen, they had to see our faith in action.

I never glorified my sins but I have been very honest with my children about the things I struggled with. They know that, before I surrendered everything to the Lord, I led a purposeless and directionless life, a very selfish existence that ultimately led to me hurting people for no other reason than to satisfy my own desires. I was being tossed to and fro. That's not the life you want to live.

We taught our kids that relationships matter most in life. Everything else pales in comparison to the relationships. You honor your spouse, you protect your children, you support your friends and, above all, you have to spend time fostering the most important relationship you have: the one with our Heavenly Father. But we could talk all we wanted; if my wife and I didn't show them what it meant to live a life committed to those values, it would never stick.

We had the same approach when we started the Northeast Ohio Basketball Association. In my years as a youth director at our church, I learned that sitting kids down for a Bible study before or after an activity rarely yields much fruit, and instead largely serves to compartmentalize faith for the kids.

I've always prayed before games, and I make sure my players understand that we aren't praying for a victory. Basketball is very small in the scheme of things and God has more important matters to deal with. Instead, I tell them, "I'm just praying that you use your abilities in a way that will glorify God, and that you would acknowledge where they come from." We pray every day at St. V before practice as well, sometimes just to say thank you for all the ways God has blessed us. But my actions have to back it up; I have to live this example out in front of them. Otherwise, I'm nothing more than a noisy gong or a clanging cymbal (1 Corinthians 13:1), preaching to a bunch of kids who'd rather be out on the basketball court.

BRON, THEN AND NOW

LeBron, in particular, latched on to the examples he saw from my coaches, my wife and me. He may be the most observant young man I have ever worked with – always listening, always watching, always taking mental notes.

As most people know, LeBron came from a single-parent home and as a young kid, he always wanted his father in his life. Carolyn and I, along with Pam and Frankie Walker (Bron's pee-wee football coach), began pouring into this young man and showing him what a family looked like and how it worked. We brought him into our homes and he saw what we did, how we treated one another, and how we were able to use basketball to influence his life and other young men's lives. We showed him that families had disagreements, that it's not always perfect, that there are sacrifices to be made, but those are the real things that life brings you. It wasn't a free ride, though; he had his share of chores to do, responsibilities that helped to finally give him a sense of purpose and belonging away from the basketball court.

I will never forget when Bron told Carolyn and me that we were his role models. We had just played a game at the Palestra in Philadelphia during his senior year, and later that night at dinner, he walked over to our table and announced that he would be just like us one day. It doesn't get more humbling than that, and I thank God for the privilege of being used to speak truth into Bron's life at such a critical age.

Today, I see that truth in action. Bron is committed to giving his family the kind of life he never had, to being the kind of father he wanted as a kid, to loving his family unconditionally and providing for them in incredible ways. I'm sure he's not around as much as he'd like because of his job, but when he has those moments at home, he makes the most of it. He's present. He appreciates the fact that, with his family, he's just Dad. He doesn't have to answer the questions in front of the cameras or perform for anyone. I know that's big for him.

He's also made a point of giving back to the community that gave so much to him through his various charitable ventures, most notably the LeBron James Family Foundation. His generosity is positively inspiring. When Bron won the Maxwell Award for the best high school athlete his senior year, I introduced him by saying, "I truly believe that he's going to do more outside of basketball than in basketball." He's fulfilled that vision and then some.

Of course, that's not to detract from the growth Bron has displayed as a player, particularly in the years since he left Cleveland for Miami. Most Cavaliers fans remember that moment as "The Decision." I like to think of it as just a necessary step in the progression of Bron's life and career.

Let's face it: the résumé of any professional athlete is ultimately judged by whether or not you have a ring. Bron was determined to win a championship, so he left in pursuit of his goals.

To be clear, I supported the decision but not necessarily "The Decision," the ESPN program that turned LeBron's announcement into a public spectacle. But while that moment admittedly could have been handled differently, the level of anger that was spewed toward Bron from the fans and the organization when he left really caught him off guard. As a kid who always just wanted to be liked – and who really is a likable guy – it certainly bothered him.

But northeast Ohio is home. His business ventures in Hollywood will probably plant him out west when he retires from the NBA, but he will always have a home here. It will always be a special place to him, so I wasn't surprised when he came back in 2014. It happened sooner than I expected, but I always knew he'd return. In the process, he displayed a level of grace and forgiveness rarely seen from professional athletes.

And boy, did he come back on a mission! He embraced the opportunity and responsibility to bring a championship to northeast Ohio, but that never would have happened if he hadn't gone to Miami. He needed to leave so he could learn from Pat Riley, Dwyane Wade and Ray Allen what it takes to be a champion. He even took a backseat to Dwyane that first year because Bron understood it was Dwyane's team, and when Dwyane moved aside and let Bron lead in their second season together, he embraced that responsibility.

THE MIRACLE

All of those experiences, those opportunities, those teaching moments and instructive examples, helped make the man who was barreling down the Oracle Arena floor last summer, chasing history down from behind. His team, once behind 3-1, knew it wouldn't be easy, but their leader refused to let them give up. And in a moment that could well define his career, Bron answered the call, squashing Iguodala's layup attempt against the glass to keep the score tied.

Dru and I are watching the game in my basement with our wives, his kids running around oblivious to what is happening on the big screen. It seems so fitting for the two of us to be there, together, on Father's Day, watching someone that we still consider part of our family accomplish something so magical. Dru and I are taking turns standing up, sitting down, standing up, sitting down. We're on pins and needles and the energy in the room is incredible. When the score stays knotted up for more than two minutes as time winds down, I want to go out there and make the basket for them. Instead, Kyrie Irving takes care of it with a new rendition of "The Shot" that Cavaliers fans are happy to see replace the Michael Jordan version from 1989.

The final seconds flip off the clock. Game over. We're jumping up and down, going crazy. It feels like our moment too, and I couldn't be more proud of the man I see on TV, celebrating with his team. Tears pour down his face, and I see a guy who is relieved. He's been carrying that pressure for years, wanting so badly to end the city's championship drought. He told the team to climb onto his back, essentially saying, "I'm going to carry this thing," and that's exactly what he did. The kid who made history by leading his high school team to four-straight state championship games, who won a state title in his final game before turning pro, who has now played in six-straight NBA Finals…. He just keeps writing great endings.

GOALS VS. DESTINY

Ephesians 3:20 tells us that God is "able to do immeasurably more than all we ask or imagine." My life stands as a testament to that. The confused, selfish and hopeless kid looking back at me from that tiny mirror inside an old trailer all those years ago never would have dreamed he could be used to accomplish so much.

Eventually, the boy in that mirror would learn that we are part of something much bigger than us, that we all have a small part to play in this grand thing we call life. In turn, I've encouraged my kids and my players to find their role, and then to play that role to the best of their abilities as they seek to fulfill God's will for their lives.

I understood early on in my coaching career that the goal may have been to win a national championship, but the destiny was to help boys grow into men. And that never ends.

———

ABOUT DRU JOYCE II

As the head boys basketball coach of St. Vincent-St. Mary in Akron, OH, Coach Dru, as he is affectionately known, has been motivator and mentor to countless young men, many of whom have played in the NBA, including LeBron James and Kosta Koufos (Sacramento Kings). Previously named *USA Today's* Coach of the Year, Coach Dru is one of the nation's most influential high school basketball coaches, having led the Fighting Irish to three state championships and a national title. Author of "Beyond Championships: A Playbook for Winning at Life," director of the Northeast Ohio Basketball Association and a 2016 inductee into the Summit County Hall of Fame, Coach Dru knows how to connect people to their potential and position themselves to win. He and his wife, Carolyn, are the proud parents of four (daughters, Ursula and India, and sons, Dru III and Cameron) and grandparents of five (Davien, Alexander, Alivia, Kanin and KJ).

WHY DADS MATTER

We love moms (hi, Mom!) and would never want to minimize the incredible sacrifices they make for their families nor the vital influence they have on their children. But because moms are so great, it seems that dads too often get a free pass. TV sitcoms and commercials love to portray fathers as selfish, lazy buffoons who are better off leaving the "real parenting" to Mom. Unfortunately, it's not all that uncommon for life to imitate art in our families today.

Through the personal stories shared in this book, we've seen examples of fathers who were purposeful about building up their kids and stoking the early flames of their faith. In the process, those fathers rejected passivity and prepared their children for the trials of life that await us all. However, some of these stories also revealed the pain that far too many carry into adulthood because their dads weren't present, weren't engaged, weren't providing the guidance they needed at the time they needed it most.

We believe these stories paint a beautiful and eclectic mosaic of the eternal significance of fatherhood, but sometimes numbers and analysis can illuminate even deeper truths. With an assist from the National Fatherhood Initiative (NFI), we have collected some sobering trends and statistics about the ways fatherlessness affects our families. Our prayer is that the stories in "Father's Day Miracle," combined with the research below, will remind us all that our kids need us to be the leaders that God created us to be in our households by embracing our purpose and being intentional with the fleeting time we have as parents.

All information taken from NFI's "Father Facts 7" publication. To learn more about the National Fatherhood Initiative, visit fatherhood.org.

*****

In America, 23.6% of children (17.4 million) lived in father-absent homes in 2014. (US Census Bureau)

In Ohio, 26.4% of homes with children under 18 are single-mother homes. In Cleveland, that number is 58.1%.

Cohabitation, divorce and nonmarital childbearing are the three primary drivers of father absence. (NFI)

About 41% of children born in the U.S. in 2012 were born to never-married parents. The percentage of births to unmarried women is more than double the percentage in 1980 (18.4%). (National Center for Health Statistics.)

In 1970, 85% of children under age 18 lived in two-parent families, 11% in single-mother families, 1% in single-father families, and 3% lived with neither parent. In 2004, by contrast, only 61% of children lived with married biological parents, 9% lived with two parents who were either unmarried or only one of whom was the child's biological parent, 23% lived with single mothers, three (3) percent with single fathers, and four (4) percent resided with neither parent—usually with grandparents or other relatives. (US Census Bureau)

In 2011, children living in female-headed homes with no spouse present had a poverty rate of 47.6%. This is over four times the rate for children living in married couple families. (US Dept of Health and Human Services)

Individuals from father absent homes were found to be 279% more likely to carry guns and deal drugs than peers living with their fathers. (Crime & Delinquency)

Father absence makes underage boys more likely to drink alcohol; father absence makes girls more likely to have early intercourse. (Various Studies)

A study of 263 13- to 18-year-old adolescent women seeking psychological services found that the adolescents from father-absent homes were 3.5 times more likely to experience pregnancy than were adolescents from father-present homes. Moreover, the rate of pregnancy among adolescents from father-absent homes was 17.4% compared to a four (4) percent rate in the general adolescent population. (Journal of Urban Health)

Ninety (90) percent of resident fathers shared a meal and spoke with their children about their children's day almost daily, 63% helped their children with homework, and 54% took their children to or from activities throughout a given week. In comparison, 31% of non-resident fathers spoke with their children about their children's day several times a week, 16% have shared a meal with their children several times a week, 10% helped with homework, and 11% took a child to or from activities. (Pew Research Center)

Adolescent boys who had dinner with their family every day were less likely to have had sex before age 16, compared with those who report they eat dinner with their family less than five nights a week. Thirty-one (31) percent of teen boys who reported having dinner with their family every day were estimated to have had sex before age 16, compared with 37% of teen boys who reported that they had dinner with their family fewer than five days a week. (Child Trends)

In 2014, more than 3.1 million children lived with cohabiting parents, which is nearly triple the 1.2 million that lived in such families in 1996. (NFI)

In 2002, about 50% of American children born to cohabiting parents experienced separation or divorce by age 9, compared to about 20% of children born to married parents. (Demographic Research)

19% of youth in stepfamilies and 16% with single parents were exposed to some form of maltreatment in 2013. Only 7% of those living with both biological parents were exposed. (Social Science and Medicine)

In a national survey of 1,533 American mothers aged 18 and older, ninety-three (93) percent agreed that there is a father absence crisis in the United States today, with 67% "strongly agreeing." (NFI)

In a separate survey of 701 American fathers aged 18 and older, ninety-one (91) percent of fathers agreed there is a father-absence crisis in the country (NFI)
7 out of 10 people surveyed believe physical absence of fathers is the most significant family or social problem currently facing America. (NFI)

By age five, nearly two-fifths of children with nonresident parents had no regular contact with their fathers for the past two years. (The Future of Children)

SPECIAL THANKS

TO RAY JESKE

Your early enthusiasm for our wild idea was so encouraging! Your helpful advice, strategic contacts and desire to see God glorified through this unique Kingdom project was over and above. Thanks so much! Twitter: @RayJeske1 / Facebook: facebook.com/ray.jeske

TO DENNIS WELCH

"I think you've got something there" were the first words I heard you say after explaining the big-picture vision of "Father's Day Miracle." Your early insights and willingness to walk us through the preliminary stages of writing a book were huge. Thanks for being the sounding board, coach and guide to a couple of rookies. http://www.bearticulate.com/

TO KENT EVANS

Thanks for returning a random call from some guy in Ohio. Your passion to help fathers build the next generation of Godly men matches the heart behind "Father's Day Miracle." There are many more stories to be written and with the resources of Manhood Journey, I pray many more dads will get in the game to disciple their kids. https://www.manhoodjourney.org/

TO OUR SUPPORTING CHURCHES

We are so thankful for your consistent prayer covering, regular financial support, and desire to impact children and families at-risk. Your support of this book is just one more way you've blessed our ministry. We couldn't do what we do without your Kingdom-minded investment. Together, we are making a difference in the next generation!

TO THE TEAM

Kevin Hewitt for buying into this adventurous project from the beginning and for supporting Jamey and me as we put countless hours of effort into it. This book wouldn't have happened without Jamey Codding. Your creative writing ability, attention to detail, and your own desire to keep growing as a dad have been a perfect fit. Thanks for going the extra mile! The rest of the team – Dan, Lauren and Jenny – thanks for carrying the load with our other projects while we pushed to publish our agency's first book.

With appreciation,

Joe Franz

Director of Advancement

Christian Children's Home of Ohio

2685 Armstrong Road

Wooster, OH 44691

330.345.7949

OUR FAMILY OF MINISTRIES

O ne young boy in need set in motion a ministry in Wooster, OH that has provided hope and healing to hundreds of children whose lives have been shattered by abuse and neglect.

In March of 1969, a serene 175-acre farm in Wooster became known as the Christian Children's Home of Ohio (CCHO) when members of the independent Christian Churches/Churches of Christ movement learned of a boy with no safe place to call home. Initially licensed as a foster/group home serving three to five children at one time, CCHO now has five cottages on its campus that are home to as many as 38 at-risk kids at once, confused and broken children who just need to know that they are loved, they are valued and they are safe.

For nearly 50 years, CCHO, Encompass Christian Counseling, and Encourage Foster Care & Adoption have helped children, adults and families cope with and recover from life's most difficult challenges. All proceeds raised by the sale of "Father's Day Miracle" will benefit Christian Children's Home of Ohio and our ministries' mission to help people experience their worth in Christ.

ccho.org • encompasscounseling.org • encouragefostercare.org

SHARE YOUR FATHER'S DAY MIRACLE STORY!

We know there are thousands of incredible stories that could have been included in this book, and that many of you reading these words have a story of your own that fits our themes of faith, fatherhood and fandom. We want to hear it!

Our prayer is that the vision and impact of the "Father's Day Miracle" project continues to grow even after the book has been released. We aren't sure what that looks like – more stories shared on fathersdaymiracle.com, a second edition of this book, maybe something bigger that we haven't even considered yet – but we trust that God will continue to lead us down this path.

If you would like to share your own "Father's Day Miracle" story for consideration in whatever future developments God has in store for this project, simply visit us online and look for the story submission page:

FATHERSDAYMIRACLE.COM